Preaching and Pa

Albert Parker Fitch

Alpha Editions

This edition published in 2024

ISBN 9789361470868

Design and Setting By

Alpha Editions

www.alphaedis.com

Email - info@alphaedis.com

As per information held with us this book is in Public Domain.
This book is a reproduction of an important historical work.
Alpha Editions uses the best technology to reproduce historical work
in the same manner it was first published to preserve its original nature.
Any marks or number seen are left intentionally to preserve.

Contents

PREFACE	- 2 -
CHAPTER ONE The Learner, the Doer and the Seer	- 3 -
CHAPTER TWO The Children of Zion and the Sons of Greece	- 18 -
CHAPTER THREE Eating, Drinking and Being Merry	- 38 -
CHAPTER FOUR The Unmeasured Gulf	- 57 -
CHAPTER FIVE Grace, Knowledge, Virtue	- 77 -
CHAPTER SIX The Almighty and Everlasting God	- 93 -
CHAPTER SEVEN Worship as the Chief Approach to Transcendence	- 109 -
CHAPTER EIGHT Worship and the Discipline of Doctrine	- 124 -

THE JAMES WESLEY COOPER MEMORIAL PUBLICATION FUND

The present volume is the fourth work published by the Yale University Press on the James Wesley Cooper Memorial Publication Fund. This Foundation was established March 30, 1918, by a gift to Yale University from Mrs. Ellen H. Cooper in memory of her husband, Rev. James Wesley Cooper, D.D., who died in New York City, March 16, 1916. Dr. Cooper was a member of the Class of 1865, Yale College, and for twenty-five years pastor of the South Congregational Church of New Britain, Connecticut. For thirty years he was a corporate member of the American Board of Commissioners for Foreign Missions and from 1885 until the time of his death was a Fellow of Yale University, serving on the Corporation as one of the Successors of the Original Trustees.

TO MY WIFE

PREFACE

The chief, perhaps the only, commendation of these chapters is that they pretend to no final solution of the problem which they discuss. How to assert the eternal and objective reality of that Presence, the consciousness of Whom is alike the beginning and the end, the motive and the reward, of the religious experience, is not altogether clear in an age that, for over two centuries, has more and more rejected the transcendental ideas of the human understanding. Yet the consequences of that rejection, in the increasing individualism of conduct which has kept pace with the growing subjectivism of thought, are now sufficiently apparent and the present plight of our civilization is already leading its more characteristic members, the political scientists and the economists, to reëxamine and reappraise the concepts upon which it is founded. It is a similar attempt to scrutinize and evaluate the significant aspects of the interdependent thought and conduct of our day from the standpoint of religion which is here attempted. Its sole and modest purpose is to endeavor to restore some neglected emphases, to recall to spiritually minded men and women certain half-forgotten values in the religious experience and to add such observations regarding them as may, by good fortune, contribute something to that future reconciling of the thought currents and value judgments of our day to these central and precious facts of the religious life.

Many men and minds have contributed to these pages. Such sources of suggestion and insight have been indicated wherever they could be identified. In especial I must record my grateful sense of obligation to Professor Irving Babbitt's *Rousseau and Romanticism*. The chapter on Naturalism owes much to its brilliant and provocative discussions.

CHAPTER ONE
The Learner, the Doer and the Seer

The first difficulty which confronts the incumbent of the Lyman Beecher Foundation, after he has accepted the appalling fact that he must hitch his modest wagon, not merely to a star, but rather to an entire constellation, is the delimitation of his subject. There are many inquiries, none of them without significance, with which he might appropriately concern himself. For not only is the profession of the Christian ministry a many-sided one, but scales of value change and emphases shift, within the calling itself, with our changing civilization. The mediaeval world brought forth, out of its need, the robed and mitered ecclesiastic; a more recent world, pursuant to its genius, demanded the ethical idealist. Drink-sodden Georgian England responded to the open-air evangelism of Whitefield and Wesley; the next century found the Established Church divided against itself by the learning and culture of the Oxford Movement. Sometimes a philosopher and theologian, like Edwards, initiates the Great Awakening; sometimes an emotional mystic like Bernard can arouse all Europe and carry men, tens of thousands strong, over the Danube and over the Hellespont to die for the Cross upon the burning sands of Syria; sometimes it is the George Herberts, in a hundred rural parishes, who make grace to abound through the intimate and precious ministrations of the country parson. Let us, therefore, devote this chapter to a review of the several aspects of the Christian ministry, in order to set in its just perspective the one which we have chosen for these discussions and to see why it seems to stand, for the moment, in the forefront of importance. Our immediate question is, Who, on the whole, is the most needed figure in the ministry today? Is it the professional ecclesiastic, backed with the authority and prestige of a venerable organization? Is it the curate of souls, patient shepherd of the silly sheep? Is it the theologian, the administrator, the prophet—who?

One might think profitably on that first question in these very informal days. We are witnessing a breakdown of all external forms of authority which, while salutary and necessary, is also perilous. Not many of us err, just now, by overmagnifying our official status. Many of us instead are terribly at ease in Zion and might become less assured and more significant by undertaking the subjective task of a study in ministerial personality. "What we are," to paraphrase Emerson, "speaks so loud that men cannot hear what we say." Every great calling has its characteristic mental attitude, the unwritten code of honor of the group, without a knowledge of which one could scarcely be an efficient or honorable practitioner within it. One of the perplexing and irritating problems of the personal life of the preacher today has to do with the collision between the secular standards of his time, this traditional code of his class, and the requirements of his faith. Shall he acquiesce in the smug conformities, the externalized procedures of average society, somewhat pietized, and join that large company of good and ordinary people, of whom Samuel Butler remarks, in *The Way of All Flesh*, that they would be "equally horrified at hearing the Christian religion doubted, or at seeing it practised?" There are ministers who do thus content themselves with being merely superrespectable. Shall he exalt the standards of his calling, accentuate the speech and dress, the code and manners of his group, the historic statements of his faith, at the risk of becoming an official, a "professional"? Or does he possess the insight, and can he acquire the courage, to follow men like Francis of Assisi or Father Damien and adopt the Christian ethic and thus join that company of the apostles and martyrs whose blood is the seed of the church? A good deal might be said today on the need of this sort of personal culture in the ministerial candidate. But, provocative and significant though the question is, it is too limited in scope, too purely subjective in nature, to suit the character and the urgency of the needs of this moment.

Again, every profession has the prized inheritance of its own particular and gradually perfected human skill. An interesting study, then, would be the analysis of that rich content of human insights, the result of generations of pastoral experience, which form the background of all great preaching. No man, whether learned or pious, or both, is equipped for the pulpit without the addition of that intuitive discernment, that quick and varied appreciation, that sane and tolerant knowledge of life and the world, which is the reward given to the friends and lovers of mankind. For the preacher deals not with the shallows but the depths of life. Like his Master he must be a great humanist. To make real sermons he has to look, without dismay or evasion, far into the heart's impenetrable recesses. He must have had some experience with the absolutism of both good and evil. I think preachers who regard sermons on salvation as superfluous have not had much experience with either. They belong to that large world of the intermediates, neither positively good nor bad, who compose the mass of the prosperous and respectable in our genteel civilization. Since they belong to it they cannot lead it. And certainly they who do not know the absolutism of evil cannot very well understand sinners. Genuine satans, as Milton knew, are not weaklings and traitors who have declined from the standards of a respectable civilization. They are positive and impressive figures pursuing and acting up to their own ideal of conduct, not fleeing from self-accepted retribution or falling away from a confessed morality of ours. Evil is a force even more than a folly; it is a positive agent busily building away at the City of Dreadful Night, constructing its insolent and scoffing society within the very precincts of the City of God.

He must know, then, that evil and suffering are not temporary elements of man's evolution, just about to be eliminated by the new reform, the last formula, the fresh panacea. To those who have tasted grief and smelt the fire such easy preaching and such confident solutions are a grave offense. They know that evil is an integral part of our universe; suffering an enduring element of the whole. So he must preach upon the chances and changes of this mortal world, or go to the house of shame or the place of mourning, knowing that there is something past finding out in evil, something incommunicable about true sorrow. They are not external things, alien to our natures, that happen one day from without, and may perhaps be avoided, and by and by are gone. No; that which makes sorrow, sorrow, and evil, evil, is their naturalness; they well up from within, part of the very texture of our consciousness. He knows you can never express them, for truly to do that you would have to express and explain the entire world. It is not easy then to interpret the evil and suffering which are not external and temporary, but enduring and a part of the whole.

So the preacher is never dealing with plain or uncomplicated matters. It is his business to perceive the mystery of iniquity in the saint and to recognize the mystery of godliness in the sinner. It is his business to revere the child and yet watch him that he may make a man of him. He must say, so as to be understood, to those who balk at discipline, and rail at self-repression, and resent pain: you have not yet begun to live nor made the first step toward understanding the universe and yourselves. To avoid discipline and to blench at pain is to evade life. There are limitations, occasioned by the evil and the suffering of the world, in whose repressions men find fulfillment. When you are honest with yourself you will know what Dante meant when he said:

"And thou shalt see those who

Contented are within the fire;

Because they hope to come,

When e'er it may be, to the blessed people."[1]

It is his business, also, to be the comrade of his peers, and yet speak to them the truth in love; his task to understand the bitterness and assuage the sorrows of old age. I suppose the greatest influence a preacher ever exercises, and a chief source of the material and insight of his preaching, is found in this intimate contact with living and suffering, divided and distracted men and women. When strong men blench with pain and exquisite grief stirs within us at the sight and we can endure naught else but to suffer with them, when youth is blurred with sin, and gray heads are sick with shame and we, then, want to die and cry, O God! forgive and save them or else blot me out of Thy book of life—for who could bear to live in a world where such things are the end!—then, through the society of sorrow, and the holy comradeship in shame, we begin to find the Lord and to understand both the kindness and the justice of His world. In the moment when sympathy takes the bitterness out of another's sorrow and my suffering breaks the captivity of my neighbor's sin—then, when because "together," with sinner and sufferer, we come out into the quiet land of freedom and of peace, we perceive how the very heart of God, upon which there we know we rest, may be found in the vicarious suffering and sacrifice called forth by the sorrow and the evil of mankind. Then we can preach the Gospel. Because then we dimly understand why men have hung their God upon the Cross of Christ!

Is it not ludicrous, then, to suppose that a man merely equipped with professional scholarship, or contented with moral conformities, can minister to the sorrow and the mystery, the mingled shame and glory of a human being? This is why the average theologue, in his first parish, is like the well-meaning but meddling engineer endeavoring with clumsy tools and insensitive fingers to adjust the delicate and complicated mechanism of a Genevan watch. And here is one of the real reasons why we deprecate men entering our calling, without both the culture of a liberal education and the learning of a graduate school. Clearly, therefore, one real task of such schools and their lectureships is to offer men wide and gracious training in the art of human contacts, so that their lives may be lifted above Pharisaism and moral self-consciousness, made acquainted with the higher and comprehensive interpretations of the heart and mind of our race. For only thus can they approach life reverently and humbly. Only thus will they revere the integrity of the human spirit; only thus can they regard it with a magnanimous and catholic understanding and measure it not by the standards of temperamental or sectarian convictions, but by what is best and highest, deepest and holiest in the race. No one needs more than the young preacher to be drawn out of the range of narrow judgments, of exclusive standards and ecclesiastical traditions and to be flung out among free and sensitive spirits, that he may watch their workings, master their perceptions, catch their scale of values.

A discussion, then, dealing with this aspect of our problem, would raise many and genuine questions for us. There is the more room for it in this time of increasing emphasis upon machinery when even ministers are being measured in the terms of power, speed and utility. These are not real ends of life; real ends are unity, repose, the imaginative and spiritual values which make for the release of self, with its by-product of happiness. In such days, then, when the old-time pastor-preacher is becoming as rare as the former general practitioner; when the lines of division between speaker, educator, expert in social hygiene, are being sharply drawn—as though new methods insured of themselves fresh inspiration, and technical knowledge was identical with spiritual understanding—it would be worth while to dwell upon the culture of the pastoral office and to show that ingenuity is not yet synonymous with insight, and that, in our profession at least, card-catalogues cannot take the place of the personal study of the human heart. But many discussions on this Foundation, and recently those of Dr. Jowett, have already dealt with this sort of analysis. Besides, today, when not merely the preacher, but the very view of the world that produced him, is being threatened with temporary extinction, such a theme, poetic and rewarding though it is, becomes irrelevant and parochial.

Or we might turn to the problem of technique, that professional equipment for his task as a sermonizer and public speaker which is partly a native endowment and partly a laborious acquisition on the preacher's part. Such was President Tucker's course on *The Making and Unmaking of the Preacher*. Certainly observations on professional technique, especially if they should include, like his, acute discussion of the speaker's obligation to honesty of thinking, no less than integrity of conduct; of the immorality of the pragmatic standard of mere effectiveness or immediate efficiency in the selection of material; of the aesthetic folly and ethical dubiety of simulated extempore speaking and genuinely impromptu prayers, would not be superfluous. But, on the other hand, we may hope to accomplish much of this indirectly today. Because there is no way of handling specifically either the content of the Christian message or the problem of the immediate needs and temper of those to whom it is to be addressed, without reference to the kind of personality, and the nature of the tools at his disposal, which is best suited to commend the one and to interpret the other.

Hence such a discussion as this ought, by its very scale of values—by the motives that inform it and the ends that determine it—to condemn thereby the insincere and artificial speaker, or that pseudo-sermon which is neither as exposition, an argument nor a meditation but a mosaic, a compilation of other men's thoughts, eked out by impossibly impressive or piously sentimental anecdotes, the whole glued together by platitudes of the Martin Tupper or Samuel Smiles variety. It is certainly an obvious but greatly neglected truth that simplicity and candor in public speaking, largeness of mental movement, what Phillips Brooks called direct utterance of comprehensive truths, are indispensable prerequisites for any significant ethical or spiritual leadership. But, taken as a main theme, this third topic, like the others, seems to me insufficiently inclusive to meet our present exigencies. It deals more with the externals than with the heart of our subject.

Again we might address ourselves to the ethical and practical aspects of preaching and the ministry. Taking largely for granted our understanding of the Gospel, we might concern ourselves with its relations to society, the detailed implications for the moral and economic problems of our social and industrial order. Dean Brown, in *The Social Message of the Modern Pulpit*, and Dr. Coffin in *In a Day of Social Rebuilding*, have so enriched this Foundation. Moreover, this is, at the moment, an almost universally popular treatment of the preacher's opportunity and obligation. One reason, therefore, for not choosing this approach to our task is that the preacher's attention, partly because of the excellence of these and other books and lectures, and partly because of the acuteness of the political-industrial crisis which is now upon us, is already focused upon it.

Besides, our present moment is changing with an ominous rapidity. And one is not sure whether the immediate situation, as distinguished from that of even a few years ago, calls us to be concerned chiefly with the practical and ethical aspects of our mission, urgent though the need and critical the pass, to which the abuses of the capitalistic system have brought both European and American society. In this day of those shifting standards which mark the gradual transference of power from one group to another in the community, and the merging of a spent epoch in a new order, neither the chief opportunity nor the most serious peril of religious leadership is met by fresh and energetic programs of religion in action. In such days, our chief gift to the world cannot be the support of any particular reforms or the alliance with any immediate ethical or economic movement. For these things at best would be merely the effects of religion. And it is not religion in its relations, nor even in its expression in character—it is the thing in itself that this age most needs. What men are chiefly asking of life at this moment is not, What ought we to do? but the deeper question, What is there we can believe? For they know that the answer to this question would show us what we ought to do.

Nor do our reform alliances and successive programs and crusades always seem to me to proceed from any careful estimate of the situation as a whole or to be conceived in the light of comprehensive Christian principle. Instead, they sometimes seem to draw their inspiration more from the sense of the urgent need of presenting to an indifferent or disillusioned world some quick and tangible evidence of a continuing moral vigor and spiritual passion to which the deeper and more potent witnesses are absent. It is as though we thought the machinery of the church would revolve with more energy if geared into the wheels of the working world. But that world and we do not draw our power from the same dynamo. And surely in a day of profound and widespread mental ferment and moral restlessness, some more fundamental gift than this is asked of us.

If, therefore, these chapters pay only an incidental attention to the church's social and ethical message, it is partly because our attention is, at this very moment, largely centered upon this important, yet secondary matter, and more because there lies beneath it a yet more urgent and inclusive task which confronts the spokesman of organized religion.

You will expect me then to say that we are to turn to some speculative and philosophic study, such as the analysis of the Christian idea in its world relationships, some fresh statement of the Gospel, either by way of apologia for inherited concepts, or as attempting to make a new receptacle for the living wine, which has indeed burst the most of its ancient bottles. Such was Principal Fairbairn's monumental task in *The Place of Christ in Modern Theology* and also Dr. Gordon's in his distinguished discussions in *The Ultimate Conceptions of Faith*.

Here, certainly, is an endeavor which is always of primary importance. There is an abiding peril, forever crouching at the door of ancient organizations, that they shall seek refuge from the difficulties of thought in the opportunities of action. They need to be continually reminded that reforms begin in the same place where abuses do, namely, in the notion of things; that only just ideas can, in the long run, purify conduct; that clear thinking is the source of all high and sustained feeling. I wish that we might essay the philosopher-theologian's task. This generation is hungry for understanding; it perishes for lack of knowledge. One reason for the indubitable decline of the preacher's power is that we have been culpably indifferent in maintaining close and friendly alliances between the science and the art, the teachers and the practitioners of religion. Few things would be more ominous than to permit any further widening of the gulf which already exists between these two. Never more than now does the preacher need to be reminded of what Marcus Aurelius said: "Such as are thy habitual thoughts, such also shall be thyself; for the soul is dyed by its thoughts."

But such an undertaking, calling for wide and exact scholarship, large reserves of extra-professional learning, does not primarily belong to a discussion within the department of practical theology. Besides which there is a task, closely allied to it, but creative rather than critical, prophetic rather than philosophic, which does fall within the precise area of this field. I mean the endeavor to describe the mind and heart of our generation, appraise the significant thought-currents of our time. This would be an attempt to give some description of the chief impulses fermenting in contemporary society, to ask what relation they hold to the Christian principle, and to inquire what attitude toward them our preaching should adopt. If it be true that what is most revealing in any age is its regulative ideas, then what is more valuable for the preacher than to attempt the understanding of his generation through the defining of its ruling concepts? And it is this audacious task which, for two reasons, we shall presume to undertake.

The first reason is that it is appropriate both to the temperament and the training of the preacher. There are three grand divisions, or rather determining emphases, by which men may be separated into vocational groups. To begin with, there is the man of the scientific or intellectual type. He has a passion for facts and a strong sense of their reality. He moves with natural ease among abstract propositions, is both critical of, and fertile in, theories; indicates his essential distinction in his love of the truth for the truth's sake. He looks first to the intrinsic reasonableness of any proposition; tends to judge both men and movements not by traditional or personal values, but by a detached and disinterested appraisal of their inherent worth. He is often a dogmatist, but this fault is not peculiar to him, he shares it with the rest of mankind. He is sometimes a literalist and sometimes a slave to logic, more concerned with combating the crude or untenable form of a proposition than inquiring with sympathetic insight into the worth of its substance. But these things are perversions of his excellencies, defects of his virtues. His characteristic qualities are mental integrity, accuracy of statement, sanity of judgment, capacity for sustained intellectual toil. Such men are investigators, scholars; when properly blended with the imaginative type they become inventors and teachers. They make good theologians and bad preachers.

Then there are the practical men, beloved of our American life. Both their feet are firmly fixed upon the solid ground. They generally know just where they are, which is not surprising, for they do not, for the most part, either in the world of mind or spirit, frequent unusual places. The finespun speculations of the philosophers and the impractical dreams of the artist make small appeal to them; the world they live in is a sharply defined and clearly lighted and rather limited place. They like to say to this man come and he cometh, and to that man go and he goeth. They are enamored of offices, typewriters, telegrams, long-distance messages, secretaries, programs, conferences and drives. Getting results is their goal; everything is judged by the criterion of effective action; they are instinctive and unconscious pragmatists. They make good cheer leaders at football games in their youth and impressive captains of industry in their old age. Their virtues are wholesome, if obvious; they are good mixers, have shrewd judgment, immense physical and volitional energy. They understand that two and two make four. They are rarely saints but, unlike many of us who once had the capacity for sainthood, they are not dreadful sinners. They are the tribe of which politicians are born but, when they are blended with imaginative and spiritual gifts, they become philanthropists and statesmen, practical servants of mankind. They make good, if conservative, citizens; kind, if uninspiring, husbands and deplorable preachers.

Then there are those fascinating men of feeling and imagination, those who look into their own hearts and write, those to whom the inner dominions which the spirit conquers for itself become a thousand-fold more real than the earth whereon they stamp their feet. These are the literary or the creative folk. Their passion is not so much to know life as to enjoy it; not to direct it, but to experience it; not even to make understanding of it an end, but only a means to interpreting it. They do not, as a rule, thirst for erudition, and they are indifferent to those manipulations of the externals of life which are dear to the lovers of executive power. They know less but they understand more than their scholastic brethren. As a class they are sometimes disreputable but nearly always unworldly; more distinguished by an intuitive and childlike than by an ingenious or sophisticated quality of mind. Ideas and facts are perceived by them not abstractly nor practically, but in their typical or symbolic, hence their pictorial and transmissible, aspects. They read dogma, whether theological or other, in the terms of a living process, unconsciously translating it, as they go along, out of its cold propositions into its appropriate forms of feeling and needs and satisfactions.

The scientist, then, is a critic, a learner who wants to analyze and dissect; the man of affairs is a director and builder and wants to command and construct; the man of this group is a seer. He is a lover and a dreamer; he watches and broods over life, profoundly feeling it, enamored both of its shame and of its glory. The intolerable poignancy of existence is bittersweet to his mouth; he craves to incarnate, to interpret its entire human process, always striving to pierce to its center, to capture and express its inexpressible ultimate. He is an egotist but a valuable one, acutely aware of the depths and immensities of his own spirit and of its significant relations to this seething world without. Thus it is both himself and a new vision of life, in terms of himself, that he desires to project for his community.

The form of that vision will vary according to the nature of the tools, the selection of material, the particular sort of native endowment which are given to him. Some such men reveal their understanding of the soul and the world in the detached serenity, the too well-defined harmonies of a Parthenon; others in the dim and intricate richness, the confused and tortured aspiration of the long-limbed saints and grotesque devils of a Gothic cathedral. Others incarnate it in gleaming bronze; or spread it in subtle play of light and shade and tones of color on a canvas; or write it in great plays which open the dark chambers of the soul and make the heart stand still; or sing it in sweet and terrible verse, full-throated utterance of man's pride and hope and passion. Some act it before the altar or beneath the proscenium arch; some speak it, now in Cassandra-tones, now comfortably like shepherds of frail sheep. These folk are the brothers-in-blood, the fellow craftsmen of the preacher. By a silly convention, he is almost forbidden to consult with them, and to betake himself to the learned, the respectable and the dull. But it is with these that naturally he sees eye to eye.

In short, in calling the preacher a prophet we mean that preaching is an art and the preacher is an artist; for all great art has the prophetic quality. Many men object to this definition of the preacher as being profane. It appears to make secular or mechanicalize their profession, to rob preaching of its sacrosanctity, leave it less authority by making it more intelligible, remove it from the realm of the mystical and unique. This objection seems to me sometimes an expression of spiritual arrogance and sometimes a subtle form of skepticism. It assumes a special privilege for our profession or a not-get-at-able defense and sanction by insisting that it differs in origin and hence in kind from similar expressions of the human spirit. It hesitates to rely on the normal and the intelligible sources of ministerial power, to confess the relatively definable origin and understandable methods of our work. It fears to trust to these alone.

But all these must be trusted. We may safely assert that the preacher deals with absolute values, for all art does that. But we may not assert that he is the only person that does so or that his is the only or the unapproachable way. No; he, too, is an artist. Hence, a sermon is not a contribution to, but an interpretation of, knowledge, made in terms of the religious experience. It is taking truth out of its compressed and abstract form, its impersonal and scientific language, and returning it to life in the terms of the ethical and spiritual experience of mankind, thus giving it such concrete and pictorial expression that it stimulates the imagination and moves the will.

It will be clear then why I have said that the task of appraising the heart and mind of our generation, to which we address ourselves, is appropriate to the preaching genius. For only they could attempt such a task who possess an informed and disciplined yet essentially intuitive spirit with its scale of values; who by instinct can see their age as a whole and indicate its chief emphases, its controlling tendencies, its significant expressions. It is not the scientist but the seer who thus attempts the precious but perilous task of making the great generalizations. This is what Aristotle means when he says, "The poet ranks higher than the historian because he achieves a more general truth." This is, I suppose, what Houston Stewart Chamberlain means when he says, in the introduction to the *Foundations of the Nineteenth*

Century: "our modern world represents an immeasurable array of facts. The mastery of such a task as recording and interpreting them scientifically is impossible. It is only the genius of the artist, which feels the secret parallels that exist between the world of vision and of thought, that can, if fortune be favorable, reveal the unity beneath the immeasurable complexities and diversities of the present order." Or as Professor Hocking says: "The prophet must find in the current of history a unity corresponding to the unity of the physical universe, or else he must create it. It is this conscious unification of history that the religious will spontaneously tends to bring about."[2]

It is then precisely the preacher's task, his peculiar office, to attempt these vast and perilous summations. What he is set here for is to bring the immeasurable within the scope of vision. He deals with the far-flung outposts, no man knows how distant, and the boundless interspaces of human consciousness; he deals with the beginning, the middle, the end—the origin, the meaning and the destiny—of human life. How can anyone give unity to such a prospect? Like any other artist he gives it the only unity possible, the unity revealed in his own personality. The theologian should not attempt to evaluate his age; the preacher may. Because the theologian, like any other scientist, analyzes and dissects; he breaks up the world. The preacher in his disciplined imagination, his spiritual intuitiveness,—what we call the "religious temperament,"—unites it again and makes men see it whole. This quality of purified and enlightened imagination is of the very essence of the preacher's power and art. Hence he may attempt to set forth a just understanding of his generation.

This brings us to the second reason for our topic namely, its timeliness. All religious values are not at all times equal in importance. As generations come and go, first one, then another looms in the foreground. But I sincerely believe that the most fateful undertaking for the preacher at this moment is that of analyzing his own generation. Because he has been flung into one of the world's transition epochs, he speaks in an hour which is radical in changes, perplexing in its multifarious cross-currents, prolific of new forms and expressions. What the world most needs at such a moment of expansion and rebellion, is a redefining of its ideals. It needs to have some eternal scale of values set before it once more. It needs to stop long enough to find out just what and where it is, and toward what it is going. It needs another Sheridan to write a new *School for Scandal*, another Swift, with his *Gulliver's Travels*, a continuing Shaw with his satiric comedies, a Mrs. Wharton with her *House of Mirth*, a Thorstein Veblen with his *Higher Learning in America*, a Savonarola with his call to repentance and indictment of worldly and unfaithful living. It is a difficult and dangerous office, this of the prophet; it calls for a considerate and honest mind as well as a flashing insight and an eager heart. The false prophet exposes that he may exploit his age; the true prophet portrays that he may purge it. Like Jeremiah we may well dread to undertake the task, yet its day and hour are upon us!

I have already spoken to this point at length, in a little book recently published. I merely add here that in a day of obvious political disillusionment and industrial revolt, of intellectual rebellion against an outworn order of ideas and of moral restlessness and doubt, an indispensable duty for the preacher is this comprehensive study and understanding of his own epoch. Else, without realizing it,—and how true this often is,—he proclaims a universal truth in the unintelligible language of a forgotten order, and applies a timeless experience to the faded conditions of yesterday.

Indeed, I am convinced that a chief reason why preaching is temporarily obscured in power, is because most of our expertness in it is in terms of local problems, of partial significances, rather than in the wider tendencies that produce and carry them, or in the ultimate laws of conduct which should govern them. We ought to be troubled, I think, in our present ecclesiastical situation, with its taint of an almost frantic immediacy. Not only are we not sufficiently dealing with the Gospel as a universal code, but, as both cause and effect of this, we are not applying it to the inclusive life of our generation. We are tinkering here and patching there, but attempting no grand evaluation. We have already granted that sweeping generalizations, inclusive estimates, are as difficult as they are audacious. Yet we have also seen that these grand evaluations are of the very essence of religion and hence are characteristic of the preacher's task. And, finally, it appears that ours is an age which calls for such redefining of its values, some fresh and inclusive moral and religious estimates. Hence we undertake the task.

There remains but one thing more to be accomplished in this chapter. The problem of the selection and arrangement of the material for such a summary is not an easy one. Out of several possible devices I have taken as the framework on which to hang these discussions three familiar divisions of thought and feeling, with their accompanying laws of conduct, and value judgments. They are the humanistic or classic; the naturalistic or primitive; and the religious or transcendent interpretation of the world and life. One sets up a social, one an individual, and one a universal standard. Under the movements which these headings represent we can most easily and clearly order and appraise the chief influences of the Protestant centuries. The first two are largely preëmpting between them, at this moment, the field of human thought and conduct and a brief analysis of them, contrasting their general attitudes, may serve as a fit introduction to the ensuing chapter.

We begin, then, with the humanist. He is the man who ignores, as unnecessary, any direct reference to, or connection with, ultimate or supernatural values. He lives in a high but self-contained world. His is man's universe. His law is the law of reasonable self-discipline, founded on observation of nature and a respect for social values, and buttressed by high human pride. He accepts the authority of the collective experience of his generation or his race. He believes, centrally, in the trustworthiness of human nature, in its group capacity. Men, as a race, have intelligently observed and experimented with both themselves and the world about them. Out of centuries of critical reflection and sad and wise endeavor, they have evolved certain criteria of experience. These summations could hardly be called eternal laws but they are standards; they are the permits and prohibitions for human life. Some of them affect personal conduct and are moral standards; some of them affect civil government and are political axioms; some of them affect production and distribution and are economic laws; some of them affect social relationships. But in every case the humanist has what is, in a sense, an objective because a formal standard; he looks without himself as an individual, yet to himself as a part of the composite experience and wisdom of his race, for understanding and for guides. Thus the individual conforms to the needs and wisdom of the group. Humanism, at its best, has something heroic, unselfish, noble about it. Its votaries do not eat to their liking nor drink to their thirst. They learn deep lessons almost unconsciously; to conquer their desires, to make light of toil and pain and discomfort; the true humanist is well aware that Spartan discipline is incomparably superior to Greek accidence. This is what one of the greatest of them, Goethe, meant when he said: "Anything which emancipates the spirit without a corresponding growth in self-mastery is pernicious."

All humanists then have two characteristics in common: first, they assume that man is his own arbiter, has both the requisite intelligence and the moral ability to control his own destiny; secondly, they place the source and criterion of this power in collective wisdom, not in individual vagary and not in divine revelation. They assert, therefore, that the law of the group, the perfected and wrought out code of human experience, is all that is binding and all that is essential. To be sure, and most significantly, this authority is not rigid, complete, fixed. There is nothing complete in the humanist's world. Experience accumulates and man's knowledge grows; the expectation and joy in progress is a part of it; man's code changes, emends, expands with his onward marching. But the humanistic point of view assumes something relatively stable in life. Hence our phrase that humanism gives us a classic, that is to say, a simple and established standard.

It is to be observed that there is nothing in humanism thus defined which need be incompatible with religion. It is not with its content but its incompleteness that we quarrel. Indeed, in its assertion of the trustworthiness of human experience, its faith in the dignity and significance of man, its respect for the interests of the group, and its conviction that man finds his true self only outside his immediate physical person, beyond his material wants and desires, it is quite genuinely a part of the religious understanding. But we shall have occasion to observe that while much of this may be religious this is not the whole of religion. For the note of universality is absent. Humanism is essentially aristocratic. It is for a selected group that it is practicable and it is a selected experience upon which it rests. Its standards are esoteric rather than democratic. Yet it is hardly necessary to point out the immense part which humanism, as thus defined, is playing in present life.

But there is another law which, from remotest times, man has followed whenever he dared. It is not the law of the group but of the individual, not the law of civilization but of the jungle. "Most men," says Aristotle, "would rather live in a disorderly than a sober manner." He means that most men would rather consult and gratify their immediate will, their nearest choices, their instantaneous desires, than conform the moment to some regulated and considerate, some comprehensive scheme of life and action. The life of unreason is their desire; the experience whose bent is determined by every whim, the expression which has no rational connection with the past and no serious consideration for the future. This is of the very essence of lawlessness because it is revolt against the normal sequence of law and effect, in mind and conduct, in favor of untrammeled adventure.

Now this is naturalism or paganism as we often call it. Naturalism is a perversion of that high instinct in mankind which issues in the old concept of supernaturalism. The supernaturalist, of a former and discredited type, believed that God violates the order of nature for sublime ends; that He "breaks into" His own world, so to speak, "revealing" Himself in prodigious, inexplicable, arbitrary ways. By a sort of degradation of this notion, a perversion of this instinct, the naturalist assumes that he can violate both the human and the divine law for personal ends, and express himself in fantastic or indecent or impious ways. The older supernaturalism exalts the individualism of the Creator; naturalism the egotism of the creature. I make the contrast not merely to excoriate naturalism, but to point out the interdependence between man's apparently far-separated expressions of his spirit, and how subtly misleading are our highly prized distinctions, how dangerous sometimes that secondary mental power which multiplies them. It sobers and clarifies human thinking a little, perhaps, to reflect on how thin a line separates the sublime and the ridiculous, the saint and the sensualist, the martyr and the fool, the genius and the freak.

Now, with this selfish individualism which we call naturalism we shall have much to do, for it plays an increasing rôle in the modern world; it is the neo-paganism which we may see spreading about us. Sophistries of all kinds become the powerful allies of this sort of moral and aesthetic anarchy. Its votaries are those sorts of rebels who invariably make their minds not their friends but their accomplices. They are ingenious in the art of letting themselves go and at the same time thinking themselves controlled and praiseworthy. The naturalist, then, ignores the group; he flaunts impartially both the classic and the religious law. He is equally unwilling to submit to a power imposed from above and without, or to accept those restrictions of society, self-imposed by man's own codified and corrected observations of the natural world and his own impulses. He jeers at the one as hypocrisy and superstition and at the other as mere "middle-class respectability." He himself is the perpetual Ajax standing defiant upon the headland of his own inflamed desires, and scoffing at the lightnings either of heaven or society. Neither devoutness nor progress but mere personal expansion is his goal. The humanist curbs both the flesh and the imagination by a high doctrine of expediency. Natural values are always critically appraised in the light of humane values, which is nearly, if not quite, the same as saying that the individual desires and delights must be conformed to the standards of the group. There can be no anarchy of the imagination, no license of the mind, no unbridled will. Humanism, no less than religion, is nobly, though not so deeply, traditional. But there is no tradition to the naturalist; not the normal and representative, but the unique and spectacular is his goal. Novelty and expansion, not form and proportion, are his goddesses. Not truth and duty, but instinct and appetite, are in the saddle. He will try any horrid experiment from which he may derive a new sensation.

Over against them both stands the man of religion with his vision of the whole and his consequent law of proud humility. The next three chapters will try to discuss in detail these several attitudes toward life and their respective manifestations in contemporary society.

Footnote 1: (return)

The Divine Comedy: Hell, canto I.

Footnote 2: (return)

The Meaning of God in Human Experience, p. 518.

CHAPTER TWO
The Children of Zion and the Sons of Greece

We are not using the term "humanism" in this chapter in its strictly technical sense. Because we are not concerned with the history of thought merely, but also with its practical embodiments in various social organizations as well. So we mean by "humanism" not only those modes and systems of thought in which human interests predominate but also the present economic, political and ecclesiastical institutions which more or less consistently express them. Hence, the term as used will include concepts not always agreeing with each other, and sometimes only semi-related to the main stream of the movement. This need not trouble us. Strict intellectual consistency is a fascinating and impossible goal of probably dubious value. Moreover, it is this whole expression of the time spirit which bathes the sensitive personality of the preacher, persuading and moulding him quite as much by its derived and concrete manifestations in contemporary society as by its essential and abstract principles.

There are then two sets of media through which humanism has affected preaching. The first are philosophical and find their expression in a large body of literature which has been moulding thought and feeling for nearly four centuries. Humanism begins with the general abstract assumption that all which men can know, or need to know, are "natural" and human values; that they have no means of getting outside the inexorable circle of their own experience.

Much, of course, depends here upon the sense in which the word "experience" is used. The assumption need not necessarily be challenged except where, as is very often the case, an arbitrarily limited definition of experience is intended. From this general assumption flows the subjective theory of morals; from it is derived the conviction that the rationalistic values in religion are the only real, or at least demonstrable, ones; and hence from this comes the shifting of the seat of religious authority from "revelation" to experience. In so far as this is a correction of emphasis only, or the abandonment of a misleading term rather than the denial of one of the areas and modes of understanding, again we have no quarrel with it. But if it means an exclusion of the supersensuous sources of knowledge or the denial of the existence of absolute values as the source of our relative and subjective understanding, then it strikes at the heart of religion. Because the religious life is built on those factors of experience that lie above the strictly rational realm of consciousness just as the pagan view rests on primitive instincts that lie beneath it. Of course, in asserting the importance of these "supersensuous" values the religionist does not mean that they are beyond the reach of human appraisal or unrelated by their nature to the rest of our understanding. By the intuitive he does not mean the uncritical nor by the supersensuous the supernatural in the old and discredited sense of an arbitrary and miraculous revelation. Mysticism is not superstition, nor are the insights of the poet the whimsies of the mere impressionist. But he insists that the humanist, in his ordinary definition of experience, ignores or denies these superrational values. In opposition to him he rests his faith on that definition of experience which underlies Aristotle's statement that "the intellect is dependent upon intuition for knowledge both of what is below and what is above itself."

Now it is this first set of factors which are the more important. For the cause, as distinguished from the occasions, of our present religious scale of values is, like all major causes, not practical but ideal, and its roots are found far beneath the soil of the present in the beginnings of the modern age in the fourteenth century. It was then that our world was born; it is of the essence of that world that it arose out of indifference toward speculative thinking and unfaith in those concepts regarding the origin and destiny of mankind which speculative philosophy tried to express and prove.

From the first, then, humanistic leaders have not only frankly rejected the scholastic theologies, which had been the traditional expression of those absolute values with which the religious experience is chiefly concerned, but also ignored or rejected the existence of those values themselves. Thus Petrarch is generally considered the first of modern humanists. He not only speaks of Rome—meaning the whole semi-political, semi-ecclesiastical structure of dogmatic supernaturalism—as that "profane Babylon" but also reveals his rejection of the distinctively religious experience itself by characterizing as "an impudent wench" the Christian church. The attack is partly therefore on the faith in transcendent values which fixes man's relative position by projecting him upon the screen of an infinite existence and which asserts that he has an absolute, that is, an other-than-human guide. Again Erasmus, in his *Praise of Folly*, denounces indiscriminately churches, priesthoods, dogmas, ethical values, the whole structure of organized religion, calling it those "foul smelling weeds of theology." It was inevitable that such men as Erasmus and Thomas More should hold aloof from the Reformation, not, as has been sometimes asserted, from any lack of moral courage but because of intellectual conviction. They saw little to choose between Lutheran, Calvinistic and Romish dogmatism. They had rejected not only mediaeval ecclesiasticism but also that view of the world founded on supersensuous values, whose persistent intimations had produced the speculative and scholastic theologies. To them, in a quite literal sense, the proper study of mankind was man.

It is hardly necessary to speak here of the attitude towards the old "supernatural" religion taken by the English Deists of the last half of the seventeenth and first half of the eighteenth century. Here was the first definite struggle of the English church with a group of thinkers who, under the leadership of Shaftesbury, Bolingbroke and others, attempted to adapt humanistic philosophy to theological speculation, to establish the sufficiency of natural religion as opposed to revelation, and to deny the unique significance of the Old and New Testament Scriptures. The English Deists were not deep or comprehensive thinkers, but they were typically humanistic in that their interests were not mainly theological or religious but rather those of a general culture. They were inconsistent with their humanism in their doctrine of a personal God who was not only remote but separated from his universe, a *deus ex machina* who excluded the idea of immanence. While less influential in England, they had a powerful effect upon French and German thinking. Both Voltaire and Rousseau were rationalists and Deists to the end of their days and both were unwearied foes of any other-than-natural sources for our spiritual knowledge and religious values.

In Germany the humanistic movement continued under Herder and his younger contemporaries, Schiller and Goethe. Its historical horizon, racial and literary sympathies, broadened under their direction, moving farther and farther beyond the sources and areas of accepted religious ideas and practices. They led the revival of study of the Aryan languages and cultures; especially those of the Hellenes and the inhabitants of the Indian peninsula. They originated that critical and rather hostile scrutiny of Semitic ideas and values in present civilization, which plays no small part in the dilettante naturalism of the moment. Thus the nature and place of *man*, under the influence of these "uninspired" literatures and cultures, became more and more important as both his person and his position in the cosmos ceased to be interpreted either in those terms of the moral transcendence of deity, or of the helplessness and insignificance of his creatures, which inform both the Jewish-Christian Scriptures and the philosophic absolutism of the Catholic theologies.

But the humanism of the eighteenth century comes most closely to grips with the classic statements and concepts of religion in the critical philosophy of Kant. It is the intellectual current which rises in him which is finding its last multifarious and minute rivulets in the various doctrines of relativity, in pragmatism, the subjectivism of the neo-realists, and in the superior place generally ascribed by present thinking to value judgments as against existential ones. His central insistence is upon the impossibility of any knowledge of God as an objective reality. Speculative reason does indeed give us the idea of God but he denies that we have in the idea itself any ground for thinking that there is an objective reality corresponding to it. The idea he admits as necessitated by "the very nature of reason" but it serves a purely harmonizing office. It is here to give coherence and unity to the objects of the understanding, "to finish and crown the whole of human knowledge."[3] Experience of transcendence thus becomes impossible. As Professor McGiffert in *The Modern Ideas of God* says: "Subjectively considered, religion is the recognition of our duties as commands of God. When we do our duty we are virtuous; when we recognize it as commanded by God we are religious. The notion that there is anything we can do to please God except to live rightly is superstition. Moreover, to think that we can distinguish works of grace from works of nature, which is the essence of historic Christianity, or that we can detect the activity of heavenly influences is also superstition. All such supernaturalism lies beyond our ken. There are three common forms of superstition, all promoted by positive religion: the belief in miracles, the belief in mysteries, and the belief in the means of grace."[4] So prayer is a confession of weakness, not a source of strength.

Kant is more than once profoundly inconsistent with the extreme subjectivism of his theory of ideas as when he says in the *Practical Reason*: "Two things fill the mind with ever new and increasing admiration and awe the oftener and the more steadily we reflect on them: the starry heavens above and the moral law within."[5] Again he remarks, "The belief in a great and wise Author of the world has been supported entirely by the wonderful beauty, order and providence, everywhere displayed in nature."[6] Here the objective reality both of what is presented to our senses and what is conceived of in the mind, is, as though unconsciously, taken for granted. Thus while he contends for a practical theism, the very basis of his interest still rests in the conviction of a Being external to us and existing independent of our thought.

But his intention of making right conduct the essence of religion is typical of the limits of humanistic interests and perceptions. In making his division of reason into the theoretical and the practical, it is to the latter realm that he assigns morality and religion. Clearly this is genuine rationalism. I am not forgetting Kant's great religious contribution. He was the son of devout German pietists and saturated in the literature of the Old Testament. It is to Amos, who may justly be called his spiritual father, that he owes the moral absoluteness of his categorical imperative, the reading of history as a moral order. He was following Amos when he took God out of the physical and put Him into the moral sphere and interpreted Him in the terms of purpose. But the doctrine of *The Critique of Practical Reason* is intended to negate those transcendent elements generally believed to be the distinctive portions of religion. God is not known to us as an objective being, an entity without ourselves. He is an idea, a belief, which gives meaning to our ethical life, a subjective necessity. He is a postulate of the moral will. To quote Professor McGiffert again: "We do not get God from the universe, we give Him to the universe. We read significance and moral purpose into it. We assume God, not to account for the world, but for the subjective need of realizing our highest good.... Religion becomes a creative act of the moral will just as knowledge is a creative act of the understanding."[2] Thus there are no ultimate values; at least we can know nothing of them; we have nothing to look to which is objective and changeless. The absolutism of the Categorical Imperative is a subjective one, bounded by ourselves, formed of our substance. Religion is not discovered, but self-created, a sort of sublime expediency. It can carry, then, no confident assertion as to the meaning and destiny of the universe as a whole.

Here, then, the nature of morality, the inspiration for character, the solution of human destiny, are not sought outside in some sort of cosmic relationship, but within, either in the experience of the superman, the genius or the hero, or, as later, in the collective experience and consciousness of the group. Thus this, too, throws man back upon himself, makes a new exaltation of personality in sharpest contrast to the scholastic doctrine of the futility and depravity of human nature. It produces the assertion of the sacred character of the individual human being. The conviction of the immeasurable worth of man is, of course, a characteristic teaching of Jesus; what it is important for the preacher to remember in humanism is the source, not the fact, of its estimate. With Jesus man's is a derived greatness found in him as the child of the Eternal; in humanism, it is, so to speak, self-originated, born of present worth, not of sublime origin or shining destiny.

So man in the humanistic movement moves into the center of his own world, becomes himself the measuring rod about whom all other values are grouped. In the place of inspiration, or prophetic understanding, which carries the implications of a transcendent source of truth and goodness, we have a sharply limited, subjective wisdom and insight. The "thus saith the Lord" of the Hebrew prophet means nothing here. The humanist is, of course, confronted with the eternal question of origins, of the thing-in-itself, the question whose insistence makes the continuing worth of the absolutist speculations. He begs the question by answering it with an assertion, not an explanation. He meets it by an exaltation of human genius. Genius explains all sublime achievements and genius is, so to speak, its own *fons et origo*. Thus Diderot says: "Genius is the higher activity of the soul."

"Genius," remarks Rousseau in a letter, "makes knowledge unnecessary." And Kant defines genius as "the talent to discover that which cannot be taught or learned."[8] This appears to be more of an evasion than a definition! But the intent here is to refer all that seems to transcend mundane categories, man's highest, his widest, his sublimest intuitions and achievements, back to himself; he is his own source of light and power.

Such an anthropocentric view of life and destiny in exalting man, of course, thereby liberated him, not merely from ecclesiastical domination, but also from those illusive fears and questionings, those remote and imaginative estimates of his own intended worth and those consequent exacting demands upon himself which are a part of the religious interpretation of life. Humanistic writing is full of the exulting sense of this emancipation. These superconsiderations do not belong in the world of experience as the humanist ordinarily conceives of it. Hence, man lives in an immensely contracted, but a very real and tangible world and within the small experimental circumference of it, he holds a far larger place (from one viewpoint, a far smaller one from another) than that of a finite creature caught in the snare of this world and yet a child of the Eternal, having infinite destinies. The humanist sees man as freed from the tyranny of this supernatural revelation and laws. He rejoices over man because now he stands,

> "self-poised on manhood's solid earth
>
> Not forced to frame excuses for his birth,
>
> Fed from within with all the strength he needs."

It is this sense of independence which arouses in Goethe a perennial enthusiasm. It is the greatest bliss, he says, that the humanist won back for us. Henceforth, we must strive with all our power to keep it.

We have attempted this brief sketch of one of the chief sources of the contemporary thought movement, that we may realize the pit whence we were digged, the quarry from which many corner stones in the present edifice of civilization were dug. The preacher tends to underestimate the comprehensive character of the pervasive ideas, worked into many institutions and practices, which are continually impinging upon him and his message. They form a perpetual attrition, working silently and ceaselessly day and night, wearing away the distinctively religious conceptions of the community. Much of the vagueness and sentimentalism of present preaching, its uncritical impressionism, is due to the influence of the non-religious or, at least, the insufficiently religious character of the ruling ideas and motives outside the church which are impinging upon it, and upon the rest of the thinking of the moment.

Now, this *abstract* humanism of the seventeenth and eighteenth centuries had a considerable influence upon early American preaching. The latter part of the eighteenth century marked a breaking away from the Protestant scholasticism of the Reformation theology. The French Revolution accented and made operative, even across the Atlantic, the typical humanistic concepts of the rights of man and the sovereignty of the individual person. Skepticism and even atheism became a fashion in our infant republic. It was a mark of sophistication with many educated men to regard Christianity as not worthy of serious consideration. College students modestly admitted that they were infidels and with a delicious naïveté assumed the names of Voltaire, Thomas Paine and even of that notorious and notable egotist Rousseau. It is said that in 1795, on the first Sunday of President administration in Yale College, only three undergraduates remained after service to take the sacrament. The reasons were partly political, probably, but these themselves were grounded in the new philosophical, anti-religious attitude.

Of course, this affected the churches. There was a reaction from Protestant scholasticism within them which, later on, culminated in Unitarianism, Universalism and Arminianism. The most significant thing in the Unitarian movement was not its rejection of the Trinitarian speculation, but its positive contribution to the reassertion of Jesus' doctrine of the worth and dignity of human nature. But it recovered that doctrine much more by the way of humanistic philosophy than by way of the teaching of the New Testament. I suppose the thing which has made the weakness of the Unitarian movement, its acknowledged lack of religious warmth and feeling, is due not to the place where it stands, but to the road by which it got there.

Yet, take it for all in all, the effect upon the preaching of the supernatural and speculative doctrines and insights of Christianity, was not in America as great as might be expected. Kant died in 1804, and Goethe in 1832, but only in the last sixty years has the preaching of the "evangelical" churches been fundamentally affected by the prevailing intellectual currents of the day. This is due, I think, to two causes. One was the nature of the German Reformation. It found preaching at a low ebb. Every great force, scholastic, popular, mystical, which had contributed to the splendor of the mediaeval pulpit had fallen into decay, and the widespread moral laxity of the clergy precluded spiritual insight. The Reformation, with its ethical and political interests, revived preaching and by the nature of these same interests fixed the limits and determined the direction within which it should develop. It is important to remember that Luther did not break with the old theological system. He continued his belief in an authority and revelation anterior, exterior and superior to man, merely shifting the locus of that authority from the Church to the Book. Thus he paved the way for Zwingli and the Protestant scholasticism which became more rigid and sterile than the Catholic which it succeeded. We usually regard the Reformation as a part of the Renaissance and hence included in the humanistic movement. Politically and religiously, it undoubtedly should be so regarded, for it was a chief factor in the renewal of German nationalism and its central doctrines of justification by faith, and the right of each separate believer to an unmediated access to the Highest, exalted the integrity and dignity of the individual. Inconsistently, however, it continued the old theological tradition. In the Lutheran system, says Paul de Lagarde, we see the Catholic scholastic structure standing untouched with the exception of a few loci. And Harnack, in the *Dogmengeschichte* calls it "a miserable duplication of the Catholic Church."

Now, New England preaching, it is true, found its chief roots in Calvinism; Calvin, rather than Luther, was the religious leader of the Reformation outside Germany. But his system, also, is only the continuation of the ancient philosophy of the Christian faith originating with Augustine. He reduced it to order, expounded it with energy and consistency, but one has only to recall its major doctrines of the depravity of man, the atonement for sin, the irresistible grace of the Holy Spirit, to see how untouched it was by the characteristic postulates of the new humanism. And it was on his theology that New England preaching was founded. It was Calvin who, through Jonathan Edwards, the elder and the younger, Joseph Bellamy, Samuel Hopkins, Nathaniel Emmons, Nathaniel N. Taylor, determined the course of the New England pulpit.

The other reason for our relative immunity from humanistic influence is accidental and complementary merely. It is the mere fact of our physical isolation, which, until the last seventy-five years, quite largely shut off thinkers here from continental and English currents of thought and contributed to the brilliant, if sterile, provincialism of the New England theology.

It is, therefore, to the second set of media, which may be generally characterized as scientific and practical, that we now turn. These are the forces which apparently are most affecting Christian preaching at this moment. But it is important to remember that a large part of their influence is to be traced to the philosophic and ethical tendencies of the earlier humanistic movement which had set the scene for them, to which they are so sympathetic that we may assert that it is in them that their practical interests are grounded and by them that their scientific methods are reinforced. I divide this second group of media, for clearness, under three heads.

First comes the rise of the natural sciences. In 1859, Darwin published the *Origin of Species* and gave to the world the evolutionary hypothesis, foreshadowed by Goethe and other eighteenth-century thinkers, simultaneously formulated by Wallace and himself. Here is a theory, open to objections certainly, not yet conclusively demonstrated, but the most probable one which we yet possess, as to the method of the appearance and the continuance of life upon the planet. It conceives of creation as an unimaginably long and intricate development from the inorganic to the organic, from simple to complex forms of life. Like Kantianism and the humanistic movement generally, the evolutionary hypothesis springs from reasoned observation of man and nature, not from any *a priori* or speculative process. With this theory, long a regulative idea of our world, preaching was forced to come to some sort of an understanding. It strikes a powerful blow at the scholastic notion of a dichotomized universe divided between nature and supernature, divine and human. It reinforced humanism by minimizing, if not making unnecessary, the objective and external source and external interpretations of religions. It pushes back the initial creative *act* until it is lost in the mists and chaos of an unimaginably remote past. Meanwhile, creative *energy*, the very essence of transcendent life, is, as we know it, not transcendent at all, but working outward from within, a part of the process, not above and beyond it. The inevitable implication here is that God is sufficiently, if not exclusively, known through natural and human media. Science recognizes Him in the terms of its own categories as in and of His world, a part of all its ongoings and developments. But His creative life is indistinguishable from, if not identical with, its expressions. Here, then, is a practical obliteration of the line once so sharply drawn between the natural and the supernatural. Hence the demarcation between the divine and human into mutually exclusive states has disappeared.

This would seem, then, to wipe out also any knowledge of absolute values. Christian theism has interpreted God largely in static, final terms. The craving for the absolute in the human mind, as witnessed by the long course of the history of thought, as pathetically witnessed to in the mixture of chicanery, fanaticism and insight of the modern mystical and occult healing sects, is central and immeasurable. But God, found, if at all, in the terms of a present process, is not static and absolute, but dynamic and relative; indefinite, incomplete, not final. And man's immense difference from Him, that sense of the immeasurable space between creator and created, is strangely contracted. The gulf between holiness and guiltiness tends also to disappear. For our life would appear to be plastic and indefinite, a process rather than a state, not open then to conclusive moral estimates; incomplete, not fallen; life an orderly process, hence not perverse but defensible; without known breaks or infringements, hence relatively normal and sufficiently intelligible.

A second factor was the rise of the humane sciences. In the seventh and eighth decades of the last century men were absorbed in the discovery of the nature and extent of the material universe. But beginning about 1890, interest swerved again toward man as its most revealing study and most significant inhabitant. Anthropology, ethnology, sociology, physical and functional psychology, came to the front. Especially the humane studies of political science and industrial economics were magnified because of the new and urgent problems born of an industrial civilization and a capitalistic state. The invention and perfection of the industrial machine had by now thoroughly dislocated former social groupings, made its own ethical standards and human problems. In the early days of the labor movement William Morris wrote, "we have become slaves of the monster to which invention has given birth." In 1853, shortly after the introduction of the cotton gin into India, the Viceroy wrote: "The misery is scarcely paralleled in the history of trade." (A large statement that!) "The bones of the cotton workers whiten the plains of India."

But the temporary suffering caused by the immediate crowding out of cottage industry and the abrupt increase in production was insignificant beside the deeper influence, physical, moral, mental, of the machine in changing the permanent habitat and the entire mode of living for millions of human beings. It removed them from those healthy rural surroundings which preserve the half-primitive, half-poetic insight into the nature of things which comes from relative isolation and close contact with the soil, to the nervous tension, the amoral conditions, the airless, lightless ugliness of the early factory settlements. Here living conditions were not merely beastly; they were often bestial. The economic helplessness of the factory hands reduced them to essential slavery. They must live where the factory was, and could work only in one factory, for they could not afford to move. Hence they must obey their industrial master in every particular, since the raw material, the plant, the tools, the very roof that covered them, were all his! In this new human condition was a powerful reinforcement, from another angle of approach, of the humanistic impulse. Man's interest in himself, which had been sometimes that of the dilettante, largely imaginative and even sentimental, was reinforced by man's new distress and became concrete and scientific.

Thus man regarded himself and his own world with a new and urgent attention. The methods and secondary causes of his intellectual, emotional and volitional life began to be laid bare. The new situation revealed the immense part played in shaping the personality and the fate of the individual by inheritance and environment. The Freudian doctrine, which traces conduct and habit back to early or prenatal repressions, strengthens the interest in the physical and materialistic sources of character and conduct in human life. Behavioristic psychology, interpreting human nature in terms of observation and action, rather than analysis and value judgments, does the same. It tends to put the same emphasis upon the external and sensationalistic aspects of human experience.

That, then, which is a central force in religion, the sense of the inscrutability of human nature, the feeling of awe before the natural processes, what Paul called the mystery of iniquity and the mystery of godliness, tends to disappear. Wonder and confident curiosity succeed humility and awe. That which is of the essence of religion, the sense of helplessness coupled with the sense of responsibility, is stifled. Whatever else the humane sciences have done, they have deepened man's fascinated and narrowing absorption in himself and given him apparent reason to believe that by analyzing the iron chain of cause and effect which binds the process and admitting that it permits no deflection or variation, he is making the further questions as to the origin, meaning and destiny of that process either futile or superfluous. So that, in brief, the check to speculative thinking and the repudiation of central metaphysical concepts, which the earlier movement brought about, has been accentuated and sealed by the humane sciences and the new and living problems offered them for practical solution. Thus the generation now ending has been carried beyond the point of combating ancient doctrines of God and man, to the place where it has become comparatively indifferent, rather than hostile, to any doctrine of God, so absorbed is it in the physical functions, the temporal needs and the material manifestations of human personality.

Finally, as the natural and humane sciences mark new steps in the expanding humanistic movement, so in these last days, critical scholarship, itself largely a product of the humanistic viewpoint, has added another factor to the group. The new methods of historical and literary criticism, of comparative investigation in religion and the other arts, have exerted a vast influence upon contemporary religious thought. They have not merely completed the breakdown of an arbitrary and fixed external authority and rendered finally invalid the notion of equal or verbal inspiration in sacred writings, but the present tendency, especially in comparative religion, is to seek the source of all so-called religious experience within the human consciousness; particularly to derive it all from group experience. Here, then, is a theory of religious origins which once more turns the spirit of man back upon itself. Robertson Smith, Jane Harrison, Durkheim, rejecting an earlier animistic theory, find the origin of religion not in contemplation of the natural world and in the intuitive perception of something more-than-world which lies behind it, but in the group experience whose heightened emotional intensity and nervous energy imparts to the one the exaltation of the many. Smith, in the *Religion of the Semites*,[2] emphasizes, as the fundamental conception of ancient religion, "the solidarity of the gods and their worshipers as part of an organic society." Durkheim goes beyond this. There are not at the beginning men and gods, but only the social group and the collective emotions and representations which are generated through membership in the group.

Here, then, is humanism again carried to the very heart of the citadel. Religion at its source contains no real perceptions of any extra-human force or person. What seemed to be such perceptions were only the felt participation of the individual in a collective consciousness which is superindividual, but not superhuman and always continuous with the individual consciousness. So that, whatever may or may not be true later, the beginning of man's metaphysical interests, his cosmic consciousness, his more-than-human contacts, is simply his social experience, his collective emotions and representations. Thus Durkheim: "We are able to say, in sum, that the religious individual does not deceive himself when he believes in the existence of a moral power upon which he depends and from which he holds the larger portion of himself. That power exists; it is society. When the Australian feels within himself the surging of a life whose intensity surprises him, he is the dupe of no illusion; that exaltation is real, and it is really the product of forces that are external and superior to the individual."[10] Yes, but identical in kind and genesis with himself and his own race. To Leuba, in his *Psychological Study of Religion*, this has already become the accepted viewpoint. Whatever is enduring and significant in religion is merely an expression of man's social consciousness and experience, his sense of participation in a common life. "Humanity, idealized and conceived as a manifestation of creative energy, possesses surprising qualifications for a source of religious inspiration." Professor Overstreet, in "The Democratic Conception of God," *Hibbert Journal*, volume XI, page 409, says: "It is this large figure, not simply of human but of cosmic society which is to yield our God of the future. There is no place in the future for an eternally perfect being and no need—society, democratic from end to end, can brook no such radical class distinction as that between a supreme being, favored with eternal and absolute perfection, and the mass of beings doomed to the lower ways of imperfect struggle."

There is certainly a striking immediacy in such language. We leave for later treatment the question as to the historical validity of such an attitude. It certainly ignores some of the most distinguished and fruitful concepts of trained minds; it rules out of court what are to the majority of men real and precious factors in the religious experience. It would appear to be another instance, among the many, of the fallacy of identifying the part with the whole. But the effect of such pervasive thought currents, the more subtle and unfightable because indirect and disguised in popular appearance and influence, upon the ethical and spiritual temper of religious leaders, the very audacity of whose tasks puts them on the defensive, is vast and incalculable. At the worst, it drives man into a mechanicalized universe, with a resulting materialism of thought and life; at the best, it makes him a pragmatist with amiable but immediate objectives, just practical "results" as his guide and goal. Morality as, in Antigone's noble phrase, "the unwritten law of heaven" sinks down and disappears. There is no room here for the Job who abhors himself and repents in dust and ashes nor for Plato's *One behind the Many*; no perceptible room, in such a world, for any of the absolute values, the transcendent interests, the ethics of idealism, any eschatology, or for Christian theodicy. That which has been the typical contribution of the religious perceptions in the past, namely, the comprehensive vision of life and the world and time *sub specie aeternitatis* is here abandoned. Eternity is unreal or empty; we never heard the music of the spheres. We are facing at this moment a disintegrating age. Here is a prime reason for it. The spiritual solidarity of mankind under the humanistic interpretation of life and destiny is dissolving and breaking down. Humanism is ingenious and reasonable and clever but it is too limited; it doesn't answer enough questions.

Before going on, in a future chapter, to discuss the question as to what kind of preaching such a world-view, seen from the Christian standpoint, needs, we are now to inquire what the effect of this humanistic movement upon Christian preaching has already been. That our preaching should have been profoundly influenced by it is inevitable. Religion is not apart from the rest of life. The very temperament of the speaker makes him peculiarly susceptible to the intellectual and spiritual movements about him. What, then, has humanism done to preaching? Has it worked to clarify and solidify the essence of the religious position? Or has preaching declined and become neutralized in religious quality under it?

First: it has profoundly affected Christian preaching about God. The contemporary sermon on Deity minimizes or leaves out divine transcendence; thus it starves one fundamental impulse in man—the need and desire to look up. Instead of this transcendence modern preaching emphasizes immanence, often to a naïve and ludicrous degree. God is the being who is like us. Under the influence of that monistic idealism, which is a derived philosophy of the humanistic impulse, preaching lays all the emphasis upon divine immanence in sharpest contrast either to the deistic transcendence of the eighteenth century or the separateness and aloofness of the God of the Hebrew Scriptures, or of the classic Greek theologies of Christianity. God is, of course; that is, He is the informing principle in the natural and human universe and essentially one with it. Present preaching does not confess this identification but it evades rather than meets the logical pantheistic conclusion. So our preaching has to do with God in the common round of daily tasks; with sweeping a room to His glory; with adoration of His presence in a sunset and worship of Him in a star. Every bush's aflame with Him; there are sermons in stones and poems in running brooks. Before us, even as behind, God is and all is well. We are filled with a sort of intoxication with this intimate and protective company of the Infinite; we are magnificently unabashed as we familiarly approach Him. "Closer is He than breathing; nearer than hands or feet." Not then by denying or condemning or distrusting the world in which we live, not by asserting the differences between God and humanity do we understand Him. But by closest touch with nature do we find Him. By a superb paradox, not without value, yet equally ineffable in sentimentality and sublime in its impiety we say, beholding man, "that which is most human is most divine!"

That there is truth in such comfortable and affable preaching is obvious; that there is not much truth in it is obvious, too. To what extent, and in what ways, nature, red with tooth and claw, indifferent, ruthless, whimsical, can be called the expression of the Christian God, is not usually specifically stated. In what way man, just emerging from the horror, the shame, the futility of his last and greatest debauch of bloody self-destruction, can be called the chief medium of truth, holiness and beauty, the matrix of divinity, is not entirely manifest. But the fatal defect of such preaching is not that there is not, of course, a real identity between the world and its Maker, the soul and its Creator, but that the aspect of reality which this truth expresses is the one which has least religious value, is least distinctive in the spiritual experience. The religious nature is satisfied, and the springs of moral action are refreshed by dwelling on the "specialness" of God; men are brought back to themselves, not among their fellows and by identifying them with their fellows, but by lifting them to the secret place of the Most High. They need religiously not thousand-tongued nature, but to be kept secretly in His pavilion from the strife of tongues. It is the difference between God and men which makes men who know themselves trust Him. It is the "otherness," not the sameness, which makes Him desirable and potent in the daily round of life. A purely ethical interest in God ceases to be ethical and becomes complacent; when we rule out the supraphenomenal we have shut the door on the chief strength of the higher life.

Second: modern preaching, under this same influence and to a yet greater degree, emphasizes the principle of identity, where we need that of difference, in its preaching about Jesus. He is still the most moving theme for the popular presentation of religion. But that is because He offers the most intelligible approach to that very "otherness" in the person of the godhead. His healing and reconciling influence over the heart of man—the way the human spirit expands and blossoms in His presence—is moving beyond expression to any observer, religious or irreligious. Each new crusade in the long strife for human betterment looks in sublime confidence to Him as its forerunner and defense. To what planes of common service, faith, magnanimous solicitude could He not lift the embittered, worldlyized men and women of this torn and distracted age, which is so desperately seeking its own life and thereby so inexorably losing it! But why is the heart subdued, the mind elevated, the will made tractable by Him? Why, because He is enough like us so that we know that He understands, has utter comprehension; and He is enough different from us so that we are willing to trust Him. In what lies the essence of the leadership of Jesus? He is not like us: therefore, we are willing to relinquish ourselves into His hands.

Now, that is only half the truth. But if I may use a paradox, it is the important half, the primary half. And it is just that essential element in the Christian experience of Jesus that modern preaching, under the humanistic impulse, is neglecting. Indeed, liberal preachers have largely ceased to sermonize about Him, just because it has become so easy! Humanism has made Jesus obvious, hence, relatively impotent. With its unified cosmos, its immanent God, its exalted humanity, the whole Christological problem has become trivial. It drops the cosmic approach to the person of Jesus in favor of the ethical. It does not approach Him from the side of God; we approach nothing from that side now; but from the side of man. Thus He is not so much a divine revelation as He is a human achievement. Humanity and divinity are one in essence. The Creator is distinguished from His creatures in multifarious differences of degree but not in kind. We do not see, then, in Christ, a perfect isolated God, joined to a perfect isolated man, in what were indeed the incredible terms of the older and superseded Christologies. But rather, He is the perfect revelation of the moral being, the character of God, in all those ways capable of expression or comprehension in human life, just because he is the highest manifestation of a humanity through which God has been forever expressing Himself in the world. For man is, so to speak, his own cosmic center; the greatest divine manifestation which we know. Granted, then, an ideal man, a complete moral being, and *ipso facto* we have our supreme revelation of God.

So runs the thrice familiar argument. Of course, we have gained something by it. We may drop gladly the old dualistic philosophy, and we must drop it, though I doubt if it is so easy to drop the dualistic experience which created it. But I beg to point out that, on the whole, we have lost more religiously than we have gained. For we have made Jesus easy to understand, not as He brings us up to His level, but as we have reduced Him to ours. Can we afford to do that? Bernard's mystical line, "The love of Jesus, what it is, none but His loved ones know," has small meaning here. The argument is very good humanism but it drops the word "Saviour" out of the vocabulary of faith. Oh, how many sermons since, let us say, 1890, have been preached on the text, "He that hath seen me, hath seen the Father." And how uniformly the sermons have explained that the text means not that Jesus is like God, but that God is like Jesus—and we have already seen that Jesus is like us! One only has to state it all to see beneath its superficial reasonableness its appalling profanity!

Third: we may see the influence of humanism upon our preaching in the relinquishment of the goal of conversion. We are preaching to educate, not to save; to instruct, not to transform. Conversion may be gradual and half-unconscious, a long and normal process under favorable inheritance and with the culture of a Christian environment. Or it may be sudden and catastrophic, a violent change of emotional and volitional activity. When a man whose feeling has been repressed by sin and crusted over by deception, whose inner restlessness has been accumulating under the misery and impotence of a divided life, is brought into contact with Christian truth, he can only accept it through a volitional crisis, with its cleansing flood of penitence and confession and its blessed reward of the sense of pardon and peace and the relinquishment of the self into the divine hands. But one thing is true of either process in the Christian doctrine of conversion. It is not merely an achievement, although it is that; it is also a rescue. It cannot come about without faith, the "will to believe"; neither can it come about by that alone. Conversion is something we do; it is also something else, working within us, if we will let it, helping us to do; hence it is something done for us.

Now, this experience of conversion is passing out of Christian life and preaching under humanistic influence. We are accepting the Socratic dictum that knowledge is virtue. Hence we blur the distinction between the Christian and the non-Christian. Education supplants salvation. We bring the boys and girls into the church because they are safer there than outside it; and on the whole it is a good thing to do and really they belong there anyway. The church member is a man of the world, softened by Christian feeling. He is a kindly and amiable citizen and an honorable man; he has not been saved. But he knows the unwisdom of evil; if you know what is right you will do it. Intelligence needs no support from grace. It is strange that the church does not see that with this relinquishment of her insistence upon something that religion can do for a man that nothing else can attempt, she has thereby given up her real excuse for being, and that her peculiar and distinctive mission has gone. It is strange that she does not see that the humanism which, since it is at home in the world, can sometimes make there a classic hero, degenerates dreadfully and becomes unreal in a church where unskilled hands use it to make it a substitute for a Christian saint! But for how many efficient parish administrators, Y.M.C.A. secretaries, up-to-date preachers, character is conceived of as coming not by discipline but by expansion, not by salvation, but by activity. Social service solves everything without any reference to the troublesome fact that the value of the service will depend upon the quality of the servant. Salvation is a combination of intelligence and machinery. Sin is pure ignorance or just maladjustment to environment. All we need is to know what is right and wrong; the humane sciences will take care of that; and, then, have an advertising agent, a gymnasium, a committee on spiritual resources, a program, a conference, a drive for money, and behold, the Kingdom of God is among us!

Fourth, and most significant: it is to the humanistic impulse and its derived philosophies that we owe the individualistic ethics, the relative absence of the sense of moral responsibility for the social order which has, from the beginning, maimed and distorted Protestant Christianity. It was, perhaps, a consequence of the speculative and absolute philosophies of the mediaeval church that, since they endeavored to relate religion to the whole of the cosmos, its remotest and ultimate issues, so they conceived of its absoluteness as concerned with the whole of human experience, with every relation of organized society. Under their regulative ideas all human beings, not a selected number, had, not in themselves but because of the Divine Sacrifice, divine significance; reverence was had, not for supermen or captains of industry, but for every one of those for whom Christ died. There were no human institutions which were ends in themselves or more important than the men which created and served them. The Holy Catholic Church was the only institution which was so conceived; all others, social, political, economic, were means toward the end of the preservation and expression of human personality. Hence, the interest of the mediaeval church in social ethics and corporate values; hence, the axiom of the church's control of, the believers' responsibility for, the economic relations of society. An unjust distribution of goods, the withholding from the producer of his fair share of the wealth which he creates, profiteering, predatory riches—these were ranked under one term as avarice, and they were counted not among the venial offenses, like aberrations of the flesh, but avarice was considered one of the seven deadly sins of the spirit. The application of the ethics of Jesus to social control began to die out as humanism individualized Christian morals and as, under its influence, nationalism tended to supplant the international ecclesiastical order. The cynical and sordid maxim that business is business; that, in the economic sphere, the standards of the church are not operative and the responsibility of the church is not recognized—notions which are a chief heresy and an outstanding disgrace of nineteenth-century religion, from which we are only now painfully and slowly reacting—these may be traced back to the influence of humanism upon Christian thought and conduct.

In general, then, it seems to me abundantly clear that the humanistic movement has both limited and secularized Christian preaching. It dogmatically ignores supersensuous values; hence it has rationalized preaching hence it has made provincial its intellectual approach and treatment, narrowed and made mechanical its content. It has turned preaching away from speculative to practical themes. It was, perhaps, this mental and spiritual decline of the ministry to which a distinguished educator referred when he told a body of Congregational preachers that their sermons were marked by "intellectual frugality." It is this which a great New England theologian-preacher, Dr. Gordon, means when he says "an indescribable pettiness, a mean kind of retail trade has taken possession of the preachers; they have substituted the mill-round for the sun-path."

The whole world today tends toward a monstrous egotism. Man's attention is centered on himself, his temporal salvation, his external prosperity. Preaching, yielding partly to the intellectual and partly to the practical environment, has tended to adopt the same secular scale of values, somewhat pietized and intensified, and to move within the same area of operation. That is why most preaching today deals with relations of men with men, not of men with God. Yet human relationships can only be determined in the light of ultimate ones. Most preaching instinctively avoids the definitely religious themes; deals with the ethical aspects of devotion; with conduct rather than with worship; with the effects, not the causes, the expression, not the essence of the religious life. Most college preaching chiefly amounts to informal talks on conduct; somewhat idealized discussions of public questions; exhortations to social service. When sermons do deal with ultimate sanctions they can hardly be called Christian. They are often stoical; self-control is exalted as an heroic achievement, as being self-authenticating, carrying its own reward. Or they are utilitarian, giving a sentimentalized or frankly shrewd doctrine of expediencies, the appeal to an exaggerated self-respect, enlightened self-interest, social responsibility. These are typical humanistic values; they are real and potent and legitimate. But they are not religious and they do not touch religious motives. The very difference between the humanist and the

Christian lies here. To obey a principle is moral and admirable; to do good and be good because it pays is sensible; but to act from love of a person is a joyous ecstasy, a liberation of power; it alone transforms life with an ultimate and enduring goodness. Genuine Christian preaching makes its final appeal, not to fear, not to hope, not to future rewards and punishments, not to reason or prudence or benevolence. It makes its appeal to love, and that means that it calls men to devotion to a living Being, a Transcendence beyond and without us. For you cannot love a principle, or relinquish yourself to an idea. You must love another living Being. Which amounts to saying that humanism just because it is self-contained is self-condemned. It minimizes or ignores the living God, in His world, but not to be identified with it; beyond it and above it; loving it because it needs to be loved; blessing it because saving it. In so doing, it lays the axe at the very root of the tree of religion. Francis Xavier, in his greatest of all hymns, has stated once for all the essence of the Christian motive and the religious attitude:

"O Deus, ego amo te

Nec amo te ut salves me

Aut quia non amantes te

Aeternis punis igne.

"Nee praemii illius spe

Sed sicut tu amasti me

Sic amo et amabo te

Solem, quia Rex meus est."

What, then, has been the final effect of humanism upon preaching? It has tempted the preacher to depersonalize religion. And since love is the essence of personality, it has thereby stripped preaching of the emotional energy, of the universal human interests and the prophetic insight which only love can bestow. Over against this depersonalization, we must find some way to return to expressing the religious view and utilizing the religious power of the human spirit.

Footnote 3: (return)

See *The Critique of Pure Reason* (Müller, tr.), pp. 575 ff.

Footnote 4: (return)

Harvard Theo. Rev., vol. I, no. 1, p. 16.

Footnote 5: (return)

The Critique of Practical Reason (tr. T.K. Abbott), p. 260.

Footnote 6: (return)

The Critique of Pure Reason, p. 702.

Footnote 7: (return)

H.T.R., vol. I, no. 1, p. 18.

Footnote 8: (return)

Anthropologie, para. 87 c.

Footnote 9: (return)

P. 32.

Footnote 10: (return)

Les Formes élémentaires de la vie religieuse, p. 322.

CHAPTER THREE
Eating, Drinking and Being Merry

We ventured to say in the preceding chapter that, under the influences of more than three centuries of humanism, the spiritual solidarity of mankind is breaking down. For humanism makes an inhuman demand upon the will; it minimizes the force of the subrational and it largely ignores the superrational elements in human experience; it does not answer enough questions. Indeed, it is frankly confessed, particularly by students of the political and economic forces now working in society, that the new freedom born in the Renaissance is, in some grave sense, a failure. It destroyed what had been the common moral authority of European civilization in its denial of the rule of the church. But for nearly four centuries it has become increasingly clear that it offered no adequate substitute for the supernatural moral and religious order which it supplanted. John Morley was certainly one of the most enlightened and humane positivists of the last generation. In his *Recollections*, published three years ago, there is a final paragraph which runs as follows: "A painful interrogatory, I must confess, emerges. Has not your school held the civilized world, both old and new alike, in the hollow of their hand for two long generations past? Is it quite clear that their influence has been so much more potent than the gospel of the various churches? *Circumspice*. Is not diplomacy, unkindly called by Voltaire the field of lies, as able as ever it was to dupe governments and governed by grand abstract catchwords veiling obscure and inexplicable purposes, and turning the whole world over with blood and tears, to a strange Witch's Sabbath?"[11] This is his conclusion of the whole matter.

But while the reasons for the failure are not far to seek, it is worth while for the preacher to dwell on them for a moment. In strongly centered souls like a Morley or an Erasmus, humanism produces a stoical endurance and a sublime self-confidence. But it tends, in lesser spirits, to a restless arrogance. Hence, both those lower elements in human nature, the nature and extent of whose force it either cloaks or minimizes, and those imponderable and supersensuous values which it tends to ignore and which are not ordinarily included in its definition of experience, return to vex and plague it. Indeed the worst foe of humanism has never been the religious view of the world upon whose stored-up moral reserves of uncompromising doctrine it has often half-consciously subsisted. Humanism has long profited from the admitted truth that the moral restraints of an age that possesses an authoritative and absolute belief survive for some time after the doctrine itself has been rejected. What has revealed the incompleteness of the humanistic position has been its constant tendency to decline into naturalism; a tendency markedly accelerated today. Hence, we find ourselves in a disintegrating and distracted epoch. In 1912 Rudolph Eucken wrote: "The moral solidarity of mankind is dissolved. Sects and parties are increasing; common estimates and ideals keep slipping away from us; we understand one another less and less. Even voluntary associations, that form of unity peculiar to modern times, unite more in achievement than in disposition, bring men together outwardly rather than inwardly. The danger is imminent that the end may be *bellum omnium contra omnes*, a war of all against all."[12]

That disintegration is sufficiently advanced so that we can see the direction it is taking and the principle that inspires it. Humanism has at least the value of an objective standard in the sense that it sets up criteria which are without the individual; it substitutes a collective subjectivism, if we may use the term, for personal whim and impulse. Thus it proclaims a classic standard of moderation in all things, the golden mean of the Greeks, Confucius' and Gautama's law of measure. It proposes to bring the primitive and sensual element in man under critical control; to accomplish this it relies chiefly upon its amiable exaggeration of the reasonableness of human nature. But the Socratic dictum that knowledge is virtue was the product of a personality distinguished, if we accept the dialogues of Plato, by a perfect harmony of thought and feeling. Probably it is not wise to build so important a rule upon so distinguished an exception!

But the positive defect of humanism is more serious. It likewise proposes to rationalize those supersensuous needs and convictions which lie in the imaginative, the intuitive ranges of experience. The very proposal carries a denial of their value-in-themselves. Its inevitable result in the humanist is their virtual ignoring. The greatest of all the humanists of the Orient was Confucius. "I venture to ask about death," said a disciple to the sage. "While you do not know life," replied he, "how can you know about death?"[13] Even more typical of the humanistic attitude towards the distinctively religious elements of experience are other sayings of Confucius, such as: "To give oneself earnestly to the duties due to men, and while respecting spiritual beings, to keep aloof from them may be called wisdom."[13] The precise area of humanistic interests is indicated in another observation. "The subjects on which the Master did not talk were ... disorder and spiritual beings."[13] For the very elements of experience which humanism belittles or avoids are found in the world where pagans like Rabelais robustly jest or the high spaces where souls like Newman meditate and pray. The humanist appears to be frightened by the one and repelled by the other; will not or cannot see life steadily and whole. That a powerful primitivistic faith, like Taoism, a sort of religious bohemianism, should flourish beside such pragmatic and passionless moderation as classic Confucianism is inevitable; that the worship of Amida Buddha, the Buddha of redemption and a future heaven, of a positive and eternal bliss, should be the Chinese form of the Indian faith is equally intelligible. After a like manner it is the humanism of our Protestant preaching today from which men are defecting into utter worldliness and indifference on the one hand and returning to mediaeval and Catholic forms of supernaturalism on the other.

For the primitive in man is a beast whom it is hard to chain nor does humanism with its semi-scientific, semi-sentimental laudation of all natural values produce that exacting mood of inward scrutiny in which self-control has most chance of succeeding. Hence here, as elsewhere on the continent, and formerly in China, in Greece and in Rome, a sort of neo-paganism has been steadily supplanting it.

To the study of this neo-paganism we now address ourselves. It is the third and lowest of those levels of human experience to which we referred in the first lecture. The naturalist, you may remember, is that incorrigible individual who imagines that he is a law unto himself, that he may erect his person into a sovereign over the whole universe. He perversely identifies discipline with repression and makes the unlimited the goal both of imagination and conduct. Oscar Wilde's epigrams, and more particularly his fables, are examples of a thoroughgoing naturalist's insolent indifference to any form of restraint. All things, whether holy or bestial, were material for his topsy-turvy wit, his literally unbridled imagination. No humanistic law of decency, that is to say, a proper respect for the opinions of mankind, and no divine law of reverence and humility, acted for him as a restraining force or a selective principle. An immediate and significant example of this naturalistic riot of feeling, with its consequent false and anarchic scale of values, is found in the film dramas of the moving picture houses. Unreal extravagance of imagination, accompanied by the debauch of the aesthetic and moral judgment, frequently distinguishes them. In screenland, it is the vampire, the villain, the superman, the saccharine angel child, who reign almost undisputed. Noble convicts, virtuous courtesans, attractive murderers, good bad men, and ridiculous good men, flit across the canvas haloed with cheap sentimentality. Opposed to them, in an ever losing struggle, are those conventional figures who stand for the sober realities of an orderly and disciplined world; the judge, the policeman, the mere husband. These pitiable and laughable figures are always outwitted; they receive the fate which indeed, in any primitive society, they so richly deserve!

How deeply sunk in the modern world are the roots of this naturalism is shown by its long course in history, paralleling humanism. It has seeped down through the Protestant centuries in two streams. One is a sort of scientific naturalism. It exalts material phenomena and the external order, issues in a glorification of elemental impulses, an attempted return to childlike spontaneous living, the identifying of man's values with those of primitive nature. The other is an emotional naturalism, of which Maeterlinck is at the moment a brilliant and lamentable example. This exchanges the world of sober conduct, intelligible and straightforward thinking for an unfettered dreamland, compounded of fairy beauty, flashes of mystical and intuitive understanding intermixed with claptrap magic, a high-flown commercialism and an etherealized sensuality.

Rousseau represents both these streams in his own person. His sentimentalized egotism and bland sensuality pass belief. His sensitive spirit dissolves in tears over the death of his dog but he bravely consigns his illegitimate children to the foundling asylum without one tremor. In his justly famous and justly infamous *Confessions*, he presents himself Satan-wise before the Almighty at the last Judgment, these *Confessions* in his hand, a challenge to the remainder of the human race upon his lips. "Let a single one assert to Thee, if he dare: I am better than that man." But his preachment of natural and spontaneous values, return to primitive conditions, was equally aggressive. If anyone wants to inspect the pit whence the Montessori system of education was digged, let him read Rousseau, who declared that the only habit a child should have is the habit of not having a habit, or his contemporary disciple, George Moore, who says that one should be ashamed of nothing except of being ashamed. There are admirable features in the schooling-made-easy system. It recognizes the fitness of different minds for different work; that the process of education need not and should not be forbidding; that natural science has been subordinated overmuch to the humanities; that the imagination and the hand should be trained with the intellect. But the method which proposes to give children an education along the lines of least resistance is, like all other naturalism, a contradiction in terms, sometimes a *reductio ad absurdum*, sometimes *ad nauseam*. As long ago as 1893, when Huxley wrote his Romanes lecture on *Evolution and Ethics*, this identity of natural and human values was explicitly denied. Teachers do not exist for the amusement of children, nor for the repression of children; they exist for the discipline of children. The new education is consistently primitivistic in the latitude which it allows to whim and in its indulgence of indolence. There is only one way to make a man out of a child; to teach him that happiness is a by-product of achievement; that pleasure is an accompaniment of labor; that the foundation of self-respect is drudgery well done; that there is no power in any system of philosophy, any view of the world, no view of the world, which can release him from the unchanging necessity of personal struggle, personal consecration, personal holiness in human life. "That wherein a man cannot be equaled," says Confucius, "is his work which other men cannot see."[14] The humanist, at least, does not blink the fact that we are caught in a serious and difficult world. To rail at it, to deny it, to run hither and thither like scurrying rats to evade it, will not alter one jot or one tittle of its inexorable facts.

Following Rousseau and Chateaubriand come a striking group of Frenchmen who passed on this torch of ethical and aesthetic rebellion. Some of them are wildly romantic like Dumas and Hugo; some of them perversely realistic like Balzac, Flaubert, Gautier, Zola. Paul Verlaine, a near contemporary of ours, is of this first number; writer of some of the most exquisite lyrics in the French language, yet a man who floated all his life in typical romantic fashion from passion to repentance, "passing from lust of the flesh to sorrow for sin in perpetual alternation." Guy de Maupassant again is a naturalist of the second sort, a brutal realist; de Maupassant, who died a suicide, crying out to his valet from his hacked throat "*Encore l'homme au rancart!*"—another carcass to the dustheap!

In English letters Wordsworth in his earlier verse illustrated the same sentimental primitivism. It would be unfair to quote *Peter Bell*, for that is Wordsworth at his dreadful worst, but even in *Tinlern Abbey*, which has passages of incomparable majesty and beauty, there are lines in which he declares himself:

"... well pleased to recognize

In nature, and the language of the sense

The anchor of my purest thought, the nurse,

The guide, the guardian of my heart, and soul

Of all my moral being."

Byron's innate sophistication saves him from the ludicrous depths to which Wordsworth sometimes fell, but he, too, is Rousseau's disciple, a moral rebel, a highly personal and subjective poet of whom Goethe said that he respected no law, human or divine, except that of the three unities. Byron's verse is fascinating; it overflows with a sort of desperate and fiery sincerity; but, as he himself says, his life was one long strife of "passion with eternal law." He combines both the romantic and the realistic elements of naturalism, both flames with elemental passion and parades his cynicism, is forever snapping his mood in *Don Juan*, alternating extravagant and romantic feeling with lines of sardonic and purposely prosaic realism.

Shelley is a naturalist, too, not in the realm of sordid values but of Arcadian fancy. The pre-Raphaelites belong here, together with a group of young Englishmen who flourished between 1890 and 1914, of whom John Davidson and Richard Middleton, both suicides, are striking examples. Poor Middleton turned from naturalism to religion at the last. When he had resolved on death, he wrote a message telling what he was about to do, parting from his friend with brave assumption of serenity. But he did not send the postcard, and in the last hour of that hired bedroom in Brussels, with the bottle of chloroform before him, he traced across the card's surface "a broken and a contrite spirit thou wilt not despise." So there was humility at the last. One remembers rather grimly what the clown says in *Twelfth Night*,

"Pleasure will be paid some time or other."

This same revolt against the decencies and conventions of our humanist civilization occupies a great part of present literature. How far removed from the clean and virile stoicism of George Meredith or the honest pessimism of Thomas Hardy is Arnold Bennett's *The Pretty Lady* or Galsworthy's *The Dark Flower*. Finally, in this country we need only mention, if we may descend so far, such naturalists in literature as Jack London, Robert Chambers and Gouverneur Morris. One's only excuse for referring to them is that they are vastly popular with the people whom you and I try to interest in sermons, to whom we talk on religion!

Of course, this naturalism in letters has its accompanying and interdependent philosophic theory, its intellectual interpretation and defense. As Kant is the noblest of the moralists, so I suppose William James and, still later, Henri Bergson and Croce are the chief protagonists of unrestrained feeling and naturalistic values in the world of thought. To the neo-realists "the thing given" is alone reality. James' pragmatism frankly relinquishes any absolute standard in favor of relativity. In *the Varieties of Religious Experience*, which Professor Babbitt tells us someone in Cambridge suggested should have had for a subtitle "Wild Religions I Have Known," he is plainly more interested in the intensity than in the normality, in the excesses than in the essence of the religious life. Indeed, Professor Babbitt quotes him as saying in a letter to Charles Eliot Norton, "mere sanity is the most Philistine and at the bottom most unessential of a man's attributes."[15] In the same way Bergson, consistently anti-Socratic and discrediting analytical intellect, insists that whatever unity may be had must come through instinct, not analysis. He refuses to recognize Plato's *One in the Many*, sees the whole universe as "a perpetual gushing forth of novelties," a universal and meaningless flux. Surrender to this eternal flux, he appears to say, and then we shall gain reality. So he relies on impulse, instinct, his *elan vital*, which means, I take it, on man's subrational emotions. We call it Intuitionism, but such philosophy in plain and bitter English is the intellectual defense and solemn glorification of impulse. "Time," says Bergson, "is a continuous stream, a present that endures."[16] Time apparently is all. "Life can have no purpose in the human sense of the word."[17] Essentially, then, James, Bergson and Croce appeal from intellect to feeling. They return to primitivism.

Here is a philosophy which obviously may be both as antihumanistic and as irreligious as any which could well be conceived. Here is license in conduct and romanticism in expression going hand in hand with this all but exclusive emphasis upon relativity in thought. Here is disorder, erected as a universal concept; the world conceived of as a vast and impenetrable veil which is hiding nothing; an intricacy without pattern. Obviously so ungoverned and fluid a universe justifies uncritical and irresponsible thinking and living.

We have tried thus to sketch that declension into paganism on the part of much of the present world, of which we spoke earlier in the chapter. It denies or ignores the humanistic law with its exacting moral and aesthetic standards; it openly flouts the attitude of obedience and humility before religious mandates, and, so far as opportunity offers or prudence permits, goes its own insolently wanton way. Our world is full of dilettanti in the colleges, anarchists in the state, atheists in the church, bohemians in art, sybarites in conduct and ineffably silly women in society, who have felt, and occasionally studied the scientific and naturalistic movement just far enough and superficially enough to grasp the idea of relativity and to exalt it as sufficient and complete in itself. Many of them are incapable of realizing the implications for conduct and belief which it entails. Others of them, who are of the lesser sort, pulled by the imperious hungers of the flesh, the untutored instincts of a restless spirit, hating Hellenic discipline no less than Christian renunciation, having no stomach either for self-control or self-surrender, look out on the mass of endlessly opposing complexities of the modern world and gladly use that vision as an excuse for abandoning what is indeed the ever failing but also the ever necessary struggle to achieve order, unity, yes, even perfection.

To them, therefore, the only way to conquer a temptation is to yield to it. They rail nonsensically at all repression, forgetting that man cannot express the full circle of his mutually exclusive instincts, and that when he gives rein to one he thereby negates another; that choice, therefore, is inevitable and that the more exacting and critical the choice, the more valuable and comprehensive the expression. So they frankly assert their choices along the lines of least resistance and abandon themselves, at least in principle, to emotional chaos and moral sentimentalism. Very often they are of all men the most meticulously mannered. But their manners are not the decorum of the humanist, they are the etiquette of the worldling. Chesterfield had these folk in mind when he spoke with an intolerable, if incisive, cynicism of those who know the art of combining the useful appearances of virtue with the solid satisfactions of vice.

Such naturalism is sometimes tolerated by those who aspire to urbane and liberal judgments because they think it can be defended on humanistic grounds. But, as a matter of fact, it is as offensive to the thoroughgoing humanist as it is to the sincere religionist. They have a common quarrel with it. Take, for example, the notorious naturalistic doctrine of art for art's sake, the defiant divorcing of ethical and aesthetic values. Civilization no less than religion must fight this. For it is as false in experience and as unclear in thinking as could well be imagined. Its defense, so far as it has any, is based upon the confusion in the pagan mind of morality with moralizing, a confusion that no good humanist would ever permit himself. Of course, the end of art is neither preaching nor teaching but delighting. For that very reason, however, art, too, must conform—hateful word!—conform to fixed standards. For the sense of proportion, the instinct for elimination, is integral to art and this, as Professor Babbitt points out, is attained only with the aid of the ethical imagination.[18] Because without the ethical restraint, the creative spirit roams among unbridled emotions; art becomes impressionism. What it then produces may indeed be picturesque, melodramatic, sensual, but it will not be beautiful because there will be no imaginative wholeness in it. In other words, the artist who divorces aesthetics from ethics does gain creative license, but he gains it at the expense of a balanced and harmonious expression. If you do not believe it, compare the Venus de Milo with the Venus de Medici or a Rubens fleshy, spilling-out-of-her-clothes Magdalen with a Donatello Madonna. When ethical restraint disappears, art tends to caricature, it becomes depersonalized. The Venus de Milo is a living being, a great personage; indeed, a genuine and gracious goddess. The Venus de Medici has scarcely any personality at all; she is chiefly objectified desire! The essence of art is not spontaneous expression nor naked passion; the essence of art is critical expression, restrained passion.

Now, such extreme naturalism has been the continuing peril and the arch foe of every successive civilization. It is the "reversion to type" of the scientist, the "natural depravity" of the older theology, the scoffing devil, with his eternal no! in Goethe's *Faust*. It tends to accept all powerful impulses as thereby justified, all vital and novel interests as *ipso facto* beautiful and good. Nothing desirable is ugly or evil. It pays no attention, except to ridicule them, to the problems that vex high and serious souls: What is right and wrong? What is ugly and beautiful? What is holy and what is profane? It either refuses to admit the existence of these questions or else asserts that, as insoluble, they are also negligible problems. To all such stupid moralizing it prefers the click of the castanets! The law, then, of this naturalism always and everywhere is the law of rebellion, of ruthless self-assertion, of whim and impulse, of cunning and of might.

You may wonder why we, being preachers, have spent so much time talking about it. Folk of this sort do not ordinarily flock to the stenciled walls and carpeted floors of our comfortable, middle-class Protestant meeting-houses. They are not attracted by Tiffany glass windows, nor the vanilla-flavored music of a mixed quartet, nor the oddly assorted "enrichments" we have dovetailed into a once puritan order of worship. That is true, but it is also true that these are they who need the Gospel; also that these folk do influence the time-current that enfolds us and pervades the very air we breathe and that they and their standards are profoundly influencing the youth of this generation. You need only attend a few college dances to be sure of that! One of the sad things about the Protestant preacher is his usual willingness to move in a strictly professional society and activity, his lack of extra-ecclesiastical interests, hence his narrow and unskillful observations and perceptions outside his own parish and his own field.

Moreover, there are other forms in which naturalism is dominating modern society. It began, like all movements, in literature and philosophy and individual bohemianism; but it soon worked its way into social and political and economic organizations. Now, when we are dealing with them we are dealing with the world of the middle class; this is our world. And here we find naturalism today in its most brutal and entrenched expressions. Here it confronts every preacher on the middle aisle of his Sunday morning congregation. We are continually forgetting this because it is a common fallacy of our hard-headed and prosperous parishioners to suppose that the vagaries of philosophers and the maunderings of poets have only the slightest practical significance. But few things could be further from the truth. It is abstract thought and pure feeling which are perpetually moulding the life of office and market and street. It has sometimes been the dire mistake of preaching that it took only an indifferent and contemptuous interest in such contemporary movements in literature and art. Its attitude toward them has been determined by temperamental indifference to their appeal. It forgets the significance of their intellectual and emotional sources. This is, then, provincialism and obtuseness and nowhere are they by their very nature more indefensible or more disastrous than in the preacher of religion.

Let us turn, then, to those organized expressions of society where our own civilization is strained the most, where it is nearest to the breaking point, namely, to our industrial and political order. Let us ask ourselves if we do not find this naturalistic philosophy regnant there. That we are surrounded by widespread industrial revolt, that we see obvious political decadence on the one hand, and a determination to experiment with fresh governmental processes on the other, few would deny. It would appear to me that in both cases the revolt and the decadence are due to that fierce, short creed of rebellion against humane no less than religious standards, which has more and more governed our national economic systems and our international political intercourse. Let me begin with business and industry as they existed before the war. I paint a general picture; there are many and notable exceptions to it, human idealism there is in plenty, but it and they only prove the rule. And as I paint the picture, ask yourselves the two questions which should interest us as preachers regarding it. First, by which of these three laws of human development, religious, humanistic, naturalistic, has it been largely governed? Secondly, by what law are men now attempting to solve its present difficulties?

The present industrial situation is the product of two causes. One of them was the invention of machinery and the discovery of steam transit. These multiplied production. They made accessible unexploited sources of raw material and new markets for finished goods. The opportunities for lucrative trading and the profitableness of overproduction which they made possible became almost immeasurable. Before these discoveries western society was generally agricultural, accompanied by cottage industries and guild trades. It was largely made up of direct contacts and controlled by local interests. After them it became a huge industrial empire of ramified international relationships.

The second factor in the situation was the intellectual and spiritual nature of the society which these inventions entered. It was, as we have seen, essentially humanistic. It believed much in the natural rights of man. The individual was justified, by the natural order, in seeking his separate good. If he only sought it hard enough and well enough the result would be for the general welfare of society. Thus at the moment when mechanical invention offered unheard-of opportunities for material expansion and lucrative business, the thought and feeling of the community pretty generally sanctioned an individualistic philosophy of life. The result was tragic if inevitable. The new industrial order offered both the practical incentive and the theoretical justification for institutional declension from humane to primitive standards. It is not to be supposed that men slipped deliberately into paganism; the human mind is not so sinister as it is stupid nor so cruel as it is unimaginative nor so brutal as it is complacent. For the most part we do not really understand, in our daily lives, what we are about. Hence society degenerated, as it always does, in the confident and stubborn belief that it was improving the time and doing God's service. But He that sitteth in the heavens must have laughed, He must have had us in derision!

For upon what law, natural, human, divine, has this new empire been founded? That it has produced great humanists is gratefully conceded; that real spiritual progress has issued from its incidental cosmopolitanism is manifest; but which way has it fronted, what have been its characteristic emphases and its controlling tendencies? Let its own works testify. It has created a world of new and extreme inequality, both in the distribution of material, of intellectual and of spiritual goods. Here is a small group who own the land, the houses, the factories, machinery and the tools. Here is a very large group, without houses, without tools, without land or goods. At this moment only 7 per cent of our 110,000,000 of American people have an income of $3,000 or more; only 1¼ per cent have an income of $5,000 or more! What law produced and justifies such a society? The unwritten law of heaven? No. The law of humanism, of Confucius and Buddha and Epictetus and Aurelius? No. The law of naked individualism; of might; force; cunning? Yes.

Here in our American cities are the overwealthy and the insolently worldly people. They have their palatial town house, their broad inland acres; some of them have their seaside homes, their fish and game preserves as well. Here in our American cities are the alien, the ignorant, the helpless, crowded into unclean and indecent tenements, sometimes 1,000 human beings to the acre. What justifies a pseudo-civilization which permits such tragic inequality of fortune? Inequality of endowment? No. First, because there is no natural inequality so extreme as that; secondly, because no one would dare assert that these cleavages in the industrial state even remotely parallel the corresponding cleavages in the distribution of ability among mankind. What justifies it, then? The unwritten law of heaven? No. The law of humanism? No. The law of the jungle? Yes.

Now for our second question. By what law, admitting many exceptions, are men on the whole trying to change this situation at once indecent and impious? This is a yet more important query. Our world has obviously awakened to the rottenness in Denmark. But where are we turning for our remedy? Is it to the penitence and confession, the public-mindedness, the identification of the fate of the individual with the fate of the whole group which is the religious impulse? Is it to a disinterested and even-handed justice, the high legalism of the Golden Rule, which would be the humanist's way? Or is it to the old law of aggression and might transferring the gain thereof from the present exploiters to the recently exploited?

It would appear to be generally true that society at this moment is not chiefly concerned with either love or justice, renunciation or discipline, not with the supplanting of the old order, but with perpetuating the naturalistic principle by means of a partial redivision of the spoils, a series of compromises, designed to make it more tolerable for one class of its former victims. Thus in capital we have the autocratic corporation, atoning for past outrages on humanity by a well-advertised benevolent paternalism, calculated to make men comfortable so that they may not struggle to be free, or by huge gifts to education, to philanthropy, to religion. In labor we see men rising in brute fury against both employer and society. They deny the basic necessities of life to their fellow citizens; they bring the bludgeon of the picket down upon the head of the scab; by means of the closed shop they refuse the right to work to their brother craftsmen; they level the incapable men up and the capable men down by insisting upon uniformity of production and wage. Thus they replace the artificial inequality of the aristocrat with the artificial equality of the proletariat, striving to organize a new tyranny for the old. It is significant that our society believes that this is the only way by which it can gain its rights. That betrays our real infidelity. For between the two, associated capital and associated labor, what is there to choose today? By what law, depending upon what sort of power, is each seeking its respective ends? By the unwritten law of heaven? No. By the humane law, some objective standard of common rights and inclusive justice? No! By the ancient law that the only effectual appeal is to might and that opportunity therefore justifies the deed? On the whole it is to this question that we must answer, yes!

Turn away now from national economics and industry to international politics. Does not its *real politik* make the philosophical naturalism of Spencer and Haeckel seem like child's play? For long there has been one code of ethics for the peaceful penetration of commercially desirable lands, for punitive expeditions against peoples possessed of raw materials, for international banking and finance and diplomatic intercourse, and another code for private honor and personal morality. There has been one moral scale of values for the father of his family and another for the same man as ward or state or federal politician; one code to govern internal disputes within the nation; another code to govern external disputes between nations. And what is this code that produced the Prussian autocracy, that long insisted on the opium trade between India and China, that permitted the atrocities in the Belgian Congo, that sent first Russia and then Japan into Port Arthur and first Germany and then Japan into Shantung, that insists upon retaining the Turk in Constantinople, that produced the already discredited treaty of Versailles? What is the code that made the deadly rivalry of mounting armaments between army and army, navy and navy, of the Europe before 1914? The code, to be sure, of cunning, of greed, of might; the materialism of the philosopher and the naturalism of the sensualist, clothed in grandiose forms and covered with the insufferable hypocrisy of solemn phrases. There are no conceivable ethical or religious interests and no humane goals or values that justify these things. International diplomacy and politics, economic imperialism, using political machinery and power to half-cloak, half-champion its ends, has no law of Christian sacrifice and no law of Greek moderation behind it. On the contrary, what should interest the Christian preacher, as he regards it, is its sheer anarchy, its unashamed and naked paganism. Its law is that of the unscrupulous and the daring, not that of the compassionate or the just. In what does scientific and emotional naturalism issue, then? In this; a man, if he be a man, will stand above divine or human law and make it operative only for the weaklings beneath. Wherever opportunity offers he will consult his own will and gratify it to the full. To have, to get, to buy, to sell, to exploit the world for power, to exploit one's self for pleasure, this is to live. The only law is the old primitive snarl; each man for himself, let the devil take the hindmost.

There is only one end to such naturalism and that is increasing anarchy. It means my will against your will; my appetite for gold, for land, for women, for luxury and beauty against your appetite; until at length it culminates in the open madness of physical violence, physical destruction, physical death and despair. There can be no other end to it. If men dare not risk being the lovers of their kind, then they must choose between being the slaves of duty or the slaves of force. What are we reading in the public prints and hearing from platform and stage? The unending wail for "rights"; the assertion of the individual. Ceased is the chant of duty, forgotten the sacrifice of love!

The events which have transformed the world since 1914 are an awful commentary upon such naturalism and a dreadful confirmation of our indictment. Before the spectacle that many of us saw on those sodden fields of Flanders, both humanist and religionist should be alike aghast. How childish not to perceive that its causes, as distinguished from its occasions, were common to our whole civilization. How perverse not to confess that beneath all our modern life, as its dominating motive, has lain that ruthless and pagan philosophy, which creates alike the sybarite, the tyrant and the anarch; the philosophy in which lust goes hand in hand with cruelty and unrestrained will to power is accompanied by unmeasured and unscrupulous force.

It is incredible to me how men can take this delirium of self-destruction, this plunging of the sword into our own heart in a final frenzy of competing anarchy and deck it out with heroic and poetic values, fling over it the seamless robe of Christ, unfurl above it the banner of the Cross! The only contribution the World War has made to religion has been to throw into intolerable relief the essentially irreligious and inhumane character of our civilization.

Of course, the men and the ideals who actually fought the contest as distinguished from the men and ideals which precipitated it and determined its movements, fill gallant pages with their heroism and holy sacrifice. For wars are fought by the young at the dictation of the old, and youth is everywhere humane and poetic. Thus, if I may be permitted to quote from a book of mine recently published:

"Our sons were bade to enter it as a 'war to end war,' a final struggle which should abolish the intolerable burdens of armaments and conscription. They were taught to exalt it as a strife for oppressed and helpless peoples; the prelude to a new brotherhood and cooperation among the nations, and to that reign of justice which is the antecedent condition of peace.

"They did their part. With adventurous faith they glorified their cause and offered their fresh lives to make it good. Their sacrifice, the idealism which lay behind it in their respective communities—the unofficial perceptions that they, the fathers and mothers and the boys, were fighting to vindicate the supremacy of the moral over the material factors of life—this has made an imperishable gift to the new world and our children's lives. When an entire commuity rises to something of magnanimity, and a nation identifies its fate with the lot of weaker states, then even mutilation and death may be gift-bringers to mankind.

"But it is more significant to our purpose to note that the blood of youth had hardly ceased to run before the officials began to dicker for the material fruits of conquest. Not how to obtain peace but how to exploit victory—to wrest each for himself the larger tribute from the fallen foe—became their primary concern. So the youth appear to have died for a tariff, perished for trade routes and harbors, for the furthering of the commercial advantages of this nation as against that, for the seizing of the markets of the world. They supposed they fought 'to end business of that sort' but they returned to find their accredited representatives contemplating universal military service in frank expectation of 'the next war.' They strove for the 'self-determination of peoples' but find that it was for some people, but not all. And as for the cooperation among nations, Judge Gary has recently told us that, as a result of the war, we should prepare for 'the fiercest commercial struggle in the history of mankind!'"[12]

Is it not clear, then, today that behind the determining as distinguished from the fighting forces of the war there lay a commercial and financial imperialism, directed by small and powerful minorities, largely supported by a sympathetic press which used the machinery of representative democracy to overthrow a more naked and brutal imperialism whose machinery was that of a military autocracy? Motives, scales of value, methods and desired ends, were much the same for all these small governing groups as they operated from behind the various shibboleths whose magic they used to nerve the arms of the contending forces. The conclusion of the war has revealed the common springs of action of the professional soldier, statesman, banker, ecclesiastic, in our present civilization. On the whole they accept the rule of physical might as the ultimate justification of conduct. They are the leaders and spokesmen in an economic, social and political establishment which, pretending to civilization, always turns when strained or imperiled by foreign or domestic dangers to physical force as the final arbiter.

It is truly ominous to see the gradual extension of this naturalistic principle still going on in the state. The coal strike was settled, not by arbitration, but by conference, and "conferences" appear to be replacing disinterested arbitration. This means that decisions are being made on the principle of compromise, dictated by the expediency of the moment, not by reference to any third party, or to some fixed and mutually recognized standards. This is as old as Pythagoras and as new as Bergson and Croce; it assumes that the concept of justice is man-made, produced and to be altered by expediences and practicalities, always in flux. But the essence of a civilization is the humanistic conviction that there is something fixed and abiding around which life may order and maintain itself.

Progress rests on the Platonic theory that laws are not made by man but discovered by him; that they exist as eternal distinctions beyond the reach of his alteration. Again, an unashamed and rampant naturalism has just been sweeping this country in the wave of mean and cruel intolerance which insists upon the continued imprisonment of political heretics, which would prohibit freedom of speech by governmental decree and oppose new or distasteful ideas by the physical suppression of the thinker. The several and notorious attempts beginning with deportations and ending with the unseating of the New York assemblymen, to combat radical thinking by physical or political persecution—attempts uniformly mean and universally impotent in history—are as sinister as they are stupid. The only law which justifies the persecution and imprisonment of religious and political heretics is neither the law of reason nor the law of love, but the law of fear, hence of tyranny and force. When a twentieth-century nation begins to raise the ancient cry, "Come now and let us kill this dreamer and we shall see what will become of his dreams," that nation is declining to the naturalistic level. For this clearly indicates that the humane and religious resources of civilization, of which the church is among the chief confessed and appointed guardians, are utterly inadequate to the strain imposed upon them. Hence force, not justice, though they may sometimes have happened to coincide, and power, not reason or faith, are becoming the embodiment of the state today.

We come now to the final question of our chapter. How has this renewal of naturalism affected the church and Christian preaching? On the whole today, the Protestant church is accepting this naturalistic attitude. In a signed editorial in the *New Republic* for the last week of December, 1919, Herbert Croly said, under the significant title of "Disordered Christianity": "Both politicians and property owners consider themselves entitled to ignore Christian guidance in exercising political and economic power, to expect or to compel the clergy to agree with them and if necessary to treat disagreement as negligible. The Christian church, as a whole, or in part, does not protest against the practically complete secularization of political, economic and social life."

You may say such extra-ecclesiastical strictures are unsympathetic and ill informed. But here is what Washington Gladden wrote in January, 1918: "If after the war the church keeps on with the same old religion, there will be the same old hell on earth that religious leaders have been preparing for centuries, the full fruit of which we are gathering now. The church must cease to sanction those principles of militaristic and atheistic nationalism by which the rulers of the earth have so long kept the earth at war."[20] Thus from within the sanctuary is the same indictment of our naturalism.

But you may say Dr. Gladden was an old man and a little extreme in some of his positions and he belonged to a past generation. But there are many signs at the present moment of the increasing secularizing of our churches. The individualism of our services, their casual character, their romantic and sentimental music, their minimizing of the offices of prayer and devotion, their increasing turning of the pulpit into a forum for political discussion and a place of common entertainment all indicate it. There is an accepted secularity today about the organization. Church and preacher have, to a large degree, relinquished their essential message, dropped their religious values. We are pretty largely today playing our game the world's way. We are adopting the methods and accepting the standards of the market. In an issue last month of the *Inter-Church Bulletin* was the following headline: "Christianity Hand in Hand with Business," and underneath the following:

"George W. Wickersham, formerly United States attorney-general, says in an interview that there is nothing incompatible between Christianity and modern business methods. A leading lay official of the Episcopal Church declares that what the churches need more than anything else is a strong injection of business method into their management. 'Some latter-day

Henry Drummond,' he said, 'should write a book on Business Law in the Spiritual World.'"

In this same paper, in the issue of March 27, 1920, there was an article commending Christian missions. The first caption ran: "Commercial Progress Follows Work of Protestant Missions," and its subtitle was "How Missionaries Aid Commerce." Here is Business Law in the Spiritual World! Here is the church commended to the heathen and the sinner as an advertising agent, an advance guard of commercial prosperity, a hawker of wares! If the *Bulletin* ever penetrates to those benighted lands of the Orient upon which we are thus anxious to bestow the so apparent benefits of our present civilization it is conceivable that even the untutored savage, to say nothing of Chinamen and Japanese, might read it with his tongue in his cheek.

Such naïve opportunism and frantic immediacy would seem to me conclusive proof of the disintegration and anarchy of the spirit within the sanctuary. It is a part of it all that everyone has today what he is pleased to call "his own religion." And nearly everyone made it himself, or thinks he did. Conscience has ceased to be a check upon personal impulse, the "thou shalt not" of the soul addressed to untutored desires, and become an amiable instinct for doing good to others. The Christian is an effusive creature, loving everything and everybody; exalting others in terms of himself. We abhor religious conventions; in particular we hasten to proclaim that we are free from the stigma of orthodoxy. We do not go to church to learn, to meditate, to repent and to pray; we go to be happy, to learn how to keep young and prosperous; it is good business; it pays. We have a new and most detestable cant; someone has justly said that the natural man in us has been masquerading as the spiritual man by endlessly prating of "courage," "patriotism"—what crimes have been committed in its name!—"development of backward people," "brotherhood of man," "service of those less fortunate than ourselves," "natural ethical idealism," "the common destinies of nations"—and now he rises up and glares at us with stained fingers and bloodshot eyes![21] In so far as we have succumbed to naturalism, we have become cold and shrewd and flexible; shallow and noisy and effusive; have been rather proud to believe anything in general and almost nothing in particular; become a sort of religious jelly fish, bumping blindly about in seas of sentiment and labeling that peace and brotherhood and religion!

Here, then, is the state of organized religion today in our churches. They are voluntary groups of men and women, long since emancipated from the control of the church as such, or of the minister as an official, set free also from allegiance to historic statements, traditional, intellectual sanctions of our faith; moulded by the time spirit which enfolds them to a half-unconscious ignoring or depreciation of what must always be the fundamental problem of religion—the relationship of the soul, not to its neighbor, but to God. Hence the almost total absence of doctrinal preaching—indeed, how dare we preach Christian doctrine to the industry and politics and conduct of this age? Hence the humiliating striving to keep up with popular movements, to conform to the moment. Hence the placid acceptance of military propaganda and even of vindictive exhortation.

Is it any wonder then that we cannot compete with the state or the world for the loyalty of men and women? We have no substitute to offer. Who need be surprised at the restlessness, the fluidity, the elusiveness of the Protestant laity? And who need wonder that at this moment we are depending upon the externals of machinery, publicity and money to reinstate ourselves as a spiritual society in the community? A well-known official of our communion, speaking before a meeting of ministers in New York City on Tuesday, March 23, was quoted in the *Springfield Republican* of the next day as saying: "The church holds the only cure for the possible anarchy of the future and offers the only preventative for the hell which we have had for the last five years. But to meet this challenge the church can only go as far—as the money permits."

Has not the time arrived when, if we are to find ourselves again in the world, we should ask, What is this religion in which we believe? What is the real nature of its resources? What the real nature of its remedies? Do we dare define it? And, if we do, would we dare to assert it, come out from the world and live for it, in the midst of the paganism of this moment? Is it true that without the loaves and the fishes we can do nothing? If so, then we, too, have succumbed to naturalism indeed!

Footnote 11: (return)

Recollections: II, p. 366 ff.

Footnote 12: (return)

Harvard Theo. Rev., vol. V, no. 3, p. 277.

Footnote 13: (return)

Analects, XI, CXI; VI, CXX.

Footnote 14: (return)

Doctrine of the Mean, ch. xxxiii, v. 2.

Footnote 15: (return)

Letter to C.E. Norton, June 30, 1904.

Footnote 16: (return)

Le Perception de Changement, 30.

Footnote 17: (return)

L'evolution creatrice, 55.

Footnote 18: (return)

Rousseau and Romanticism, p. 206.

Footnote 19: (return)

Can the Church Survive? pp. 14 ff.

Footnote 20: (return)

The *Pacific*, January 17, 1918.

Footnote 21: (return)

Rousseau and Romanticism, p. 376.

CHAPTER FOUR
The Unmeasured Gulf

You may remember that when Daniel Webster made his reply to Hayne in the Senate he began the argument by a return to first principles. "When the mariner," said he, "has been tossed for many days in thick weather and on an unknown sea, he naturally avails himself of the first pause in the storm, the earliest glance of the sun, to take his latitude, and ascertain how far the elements have driven him from his true course. Let us imitate this prudence and before we float further on the waves of this debate, refer to the point from which we departed." He then asked for the reading of the resolution.

It is to some such rehearsing of our original message, a restatement of the thesis which we, as preachers, are set to commend, that we turn ourselves in these pages. The brutal dislocations of the war, and the long and confused course of disintegrating life that lay behind it, have driven civilization from its true course and deflected the church from her normal path, her natural undertakings. Let us try, then, to get back to our charter; define once more what we really stand for; view our human life, not as captain of industry, or international politician, or pagan worldling, or even classic hero, would regard it, but see it through the eyes of a Paul, an Augustine, a Bernard, a Luther, the Lord Jesus. We have already remarked how timely and necessary is this redefining of our religious values. If, as Lessing said, it is the end of education to make men to see things that are large as large and things that are small as small, it is even more truly the end of Christian preaching. What we are most in need of today is a corrected perspective of our faith; without it we darken counsel as we talk in confusion. So, while we may not attempt here a detailed and reasoned statement of religious belief, we may try to say what is the fundamental attitude, both toward nature and toward man, that lies underneath the religious experience. We have seen that we are not stating that attitude very clearly nowadays in our pulpits; hence we are often dealing there with sentimental or stereotyped or humane or even pagan interpretations. Yet nothing is more fatal for us; if we peddle other men's wares they will be very sure that we despise our own.

We approach, then, the third and final level of experience to which we referred in the first lecture. We have seen that the humanist accepts the law of measure; he rests back upon the selected and certified experience of his race; from within himself, as the noblest inhabitant of the planet, and by the further critical observation of nature he proposes to interpret and guide his life. He is convinced that this combined authority of reason and observation will lead to the *summum bonum* of the golden mean in which unbridled self-expression will be seen as equally unwise and indecent and ascetic repression as both unworthy and unnecessary. It is important to again remind ourselves that confidence in the human spirit as the master of its own fate, and in reason and natural observation as offering it the means of this self-control and understanding, are essential humanistic principles. The humanist world is rational, social, ethical.

Over against this reasonable and disciplined view of man and of his world stands naturalism. It exploits the defects of the classic "virtue"; it is, so to speak, humanism run to seed. Just as religion so often sinks into bigotry, cruelty and superstitition, so humanism, in lesser souls, declines to egotism, license and sentimentality. Naturalism, either by a shallow and insincere use of the materialistic view of the universe, or by the exalting of wanton feeling and whimsical fancy as ends in themselves, attempts the identification of man with the natural order, permits him to conceive of each desire, instinct, impulse, as, being natural, thereby defensible and valuable. Hence it permits him to disregard the imposed laws of civilization—those fixed points of a humane order—and to return in principle, and so far as he dares in action, to the unlimited and irresponsible individualism of the horde. Inevitably the law of the jungle is deliberately exalted, or unconsciously adopted, over against the humanist law of moderation and discipline.

The humanist, then, critically studies nature and mankind, finding in her matrix and in his own spirit data for the guidance of the race, improving upon it by a cultivated and collective experience. The naturalist uncritically exalts nature, seeks identification with it so that he may freely exploit both himself and it. The faith of the one is in the self-sufficiency of the disciplined spirit of mankind; the unfaith of the other is in its glorification of the natural world and in its allegiance to the momentary devices and desires of the separate heart. It will be borne in mind that these definitions are too clear-cut; that these divisions appear in the complexities of human experience, blurred and modified by the welter of cross currents, subsidiary conflicting movements, which obscure all human problems. They represent genuine and significant divisions of thought and conduct. But they appear in actual experience as controlling emphases rather than mutually exclusive territories.

Now, the clearest way to get before us the religious view of the world and the law which issues from it is to contrast it with the other two. In the first place, the religious temperament takes a very different view of nature than either romantic, or to a less degree scientific, naturalism. Naturalism is subrational on the one hand or non-imaginative on the other, in that it emphasizes the *continuity* between man and the physical universe. The religious man is superrational and nobly imaginative as he emphasizes the *difference* between man and nature. He does not forget man's biological kinship to the brute, his intimate structural and even psychological relation to the primates, but he is aware that it is not in dwelling upon these facts that his spirit discovers what is distinctive to man as man. That he believes will be found by accenting the *chasm* between man and nature. He does not know how to conceive of a personal being except by thinking of him as proceeding by other, though not conflicting, laws and by moving toward different secondary ends from those laws and ends which govern the impersonal external world. This sense of the difference between man and nature he shares with the humanist, only the humanist does not carry it as far as he does and hence may not draw from it his ultimate conclusions.

The religious view, then, begins with the perception of man's isolation in the natural order; his difference from his surroundings. That sense of separateness is fundamental to the religious nature. The false sentiment and partial science of the pagan which stresses the identification of man and beast is the first quarrel that religionist and humanist alike have with him. Neither of them sanctions this perversion of thought and feeling which either projects the impressionistic self so absurdly and perilously into the natural order, or else minimizes man's imaginative and intellectual power, leveling him down to the amoral instinct of the brute. "How much more," said Jesus, "is a man better than a sheep!" One of the greatest of English humanists was Matthew Arnold. You remember his sonnet, entitled, alas! "To a Preacher," which runs as follows:

"In harmony with Nature? Restless fool,

Who with such heat doth preach what were to thee,

When true, the last impossibility—

To be like Nature strong, like Nature cool!

Know, man hath all which Nature hath, but more,

And in that more lie all his hopes of good,

Nature is cruel, man is sick of blood;

Nature is stubborn, man would fain adore;

Nature is fickle, man hath need of rest;

Nature forgives no debt and fears no grave;

Man would be mild, and with safe conscience blest.

Man must begin; know this, where Nature ends;

Nature and man can never be fast friends.

Fool, if thou canst not pass her, rest her slave!"

Religionist and humanist alike share this clear sense of separateness. Literature is full of the expression of it. Religion, in especial, has little to do with the natural world as such. It is that other and inner one, which can make a hell of heaven, a heaven of hell, with which it is chiefly concerned. Who can forget Othello's soliloquy as he prepares to darken his marriage chamber before the murder of his wife?

"Put out the light, and then put out the light.

If I quench thee, thou flaming minister,

I can again thy former light restore,

Should I repent me; but once put out thy light,

Thou cunning'st pattern of excelling nature,

I know not where is that Promethean heat,

That can thy light relume. When I have pluck'd the rose

I cannot give it vital growth again,

It needs must wither."

Indeed, how vivid to us all is this difference between man and nature. "I would to heaven," Byron traced on the back of the manuscript of *Don Juan*,

"I would to heaven that I were so much clay,

As I am bone, blood, marrow, passion, feeling."

Ah me! So at many times would most of us. And in that sense that we are not is where the religious consciousness takes its beginning.

Here is the sense of the gap between man and the natural world felt because man has no power over it. He cannot swerve nor modify its laws, nor do his laws acknowledge its ascendency over them. But what makes the gulf deeper is the sense of the immeasurable moral difference between a thinking, feeling, self-estimating being and all this unheeding world about him. Whatever it is that looks out from the windows of our eyes something not merely of wonder and desire but also of fear and repulsion must be there as it gazes into so cruel as well as so alien an environment. For a moral being to glorify nature as such is pure folly or sheer sentimentality. For he knows that her apparent repose and beauty is built up on the ruthless and unending warfare of matched forces, it represents a dreadful equilibrium of pain. He knows, too, that that in him which allies him with this natural world is his baser, not his better part. This nobly pessimistic attitude toward the natural universe and toward man so far as he shares in its characteristics, is found in all classic systems of theology and has dominated the greater part of Christian thinking. If it is ignored today by the pseudo-religionists and the sentimentalists; it is clearly enough perceived by contemporary science and contemporary art. The biologist understands it. "I know of no study," wrote Thomas Huxley, "which is so unutterably saddening as that of the evolution of humanity as set forth in the annals of history. Out of the darkness of prehistoric ages man emerges with the marks of his lowly origin strong upon him. He is a brute, only more intelligent than the other brutes; a blind prey to impulses which as often as not lead him to destruction; a victim to endless illusions which make his mental existence a terror and a burden, and fill his physical life with barren toil and battle. He attains a certain degree of comfort, and develops a more or less workable theory of life in such favorable situations as the plains of Mesopotamia or of Egypt, and then, for thousands and thousands of years struggles with various fortunes, attended by infinite wickedness, bloodshed and misery, to maintain himself at this point against the greed and ambition of his fellow men. He makes a point of killing and otherwise persecuting all those who first try to get him to move on; and when he has moved a step farther he foolishly confers post-mortem deification on his victims. He exactly repeats the process with all who want to move a step yet farther."[22]

And no less does the artist, the man of high and correct feeling, perceive the immeasurable distance between uncaring nature and suffering men and women. There is, for instance, the passage in *The Education of Henry Adams*, in which Adams speaks of the death of his sister at Bagni di Lucca. "In the singular color of the Tuscan atmosphere, the hills and vineyards of the Apennines seemed bursting with midsummer blood. The sick room itself glowed with the Italian joy of life; friends filled it; no harsh northern lights pierced the soft shadows; even the dying woman shared the sense of the Italian summer, the soft velvet air, the humor, the courage, the sensual fullness of Nature and man. She faced death, as women mostly do, bravely and even gayly, racked slowly to unconsciousness but yielding only to violence, as a soldier sabred in battle. For many thousands of years, on these hills and plains, Nature had gone on sabring men and women with the same air of sensual pleasure.

"Impressions like these are not reasoned or catalogued in the mind; they are felt as a part of violent emotion; and the mind that feels them is a different one from that which reasons; it is thought of a different power and a different person. The first serious consciousness of Nature's gesture—her attitude toward life—took form then as a phantasm, a nightmare, an insanity of force. For the first time the stage scenery of the senses collapsed; the human mind felt itself stripped naked, vibrating in a void of shapeless energies, with resistless mass, colliding, crushing, wasting and destroying what these same energies had created and labored from eternity to perfect."

Here is a vivid interpretation of a universal human experience. Might not any one of us who had endured it turn upon the pagan and sentimentalist, crying in the mood of a Swift or a Voltaire, "*Ca vous amuse, la vie*"? The abstract natural rights of the eighteenth century smack of academic complacency before this. The indignation we feel against the insolent individualism of a Louis XIV who cried "*L'état c'est moi*!" or against the industrial overlord who spills the tears of women for his ambition, the sweat of the children for his greed, is as nothing beside the indignation with the natural order which any biological study would arouse except as the scientist perceives that indignation is, for him, beside the point and the religionist believes that it proceeds from not seeing far enough into the process. This is why there is an essential absurdity in any naturalistic system of ethics. Even the clown can say,

"Here's a night that pities

Neither wise men nor fools."

This common attitude of the religionist toward nature as a remote and cruel world, alien to our spirits, is abundantly reflected in literature. It finds a sort of final consummation in the intuitive insight, the bright understanding of the creative spirits of our race. What Aristotle defines as the tragic emotions, the sense of the terror and the pity of human life, arise partly from this perception of the isolation always and keenly felt by dramatist and prophet and poet. They know well that Nature does not exist by our law; that we neither control nor understand it; is it not our friend?

There is, then, the law of identity between man and nature, found in their common physical origin; there is also the law of difference. It is on that aspect of reality that religion places its emphasis. It is with this approach to understanding ourselves that preachers, as distinguished from scientists, deal. Our present society is traveling farther and farther away from reality in so far as it turns either to the outside world of fact, or to the domain of natural law, expecting to find in these the elements of insight for the fresh guidance of the human spirit. Not there resides the secret of the beings of whom Shelley said,

"We look before and after

And pine for what is not,

Our sincerest laughter

With some pain is fraught."

Instinct is a base, a prime factor, part of the matrix of personality. But personality is not instinct; it is instinct plus a different force; instinct transformed by spiritual insight and controlled by moral discipline. The man of religion, therefore, finds himself not in one but two worlds, not indeed mutually exclusive, having a common origin, but nevertheless significantly distinct. Each is incomplete without the other, each in a true sense non-existent without the other. But that which is most vital to man's world is unknown in the domain of nature. Already the perception of a dualism is here.

But now a third element comes into it. There is something spiritually common to nature and man behind the one, within the other. This Something is the origin, the responsible agent for man's and nature's physical identity. This Something binds the separates into a sort of whole. This, I suppose, is what Professor Hocking refers to when he says, "the original source of the knowledge of God is an experience which might be described as of *not being alone in knowing the world*, and especially the world of nature."[23] Thus the religious man recognizes beyond the gulf, behind the chasm, something more like himself than it. When he contemplates nature, he sees something other than nature; not a world which is what it seems to be, but a world whose chief significance is that it is more than it seems to be. It is a world where appearance and reality are inextricably mingled and yet sublimely and significantly separate. In short, the naturalist, the pagan, takes the world as it stands; it is just what it appears; the essence of his irreligion is that he perceives nothing in it that needs to be explained. But the religionist knows that the world which lies before our mortal vision so splendid and so ruthless, so beautiful and so dreadful, does really gain both its substance and significance from immaterial and unseen powers. It is significant not in itself but because it hides the truth. It points forever to a beyond. It is the vague and insubstantial pageant of a dream. Behind it, within the impenetrable shadows, stands the Infinite Watcher of the sons of men.

In every age religious souls have voiced this unearthliness of reality, the noble other-worldliness of the goals of the natural order. "Heard melodies are sweet, but unheard melodies are sweeter." Poet, philosopher and mystic have sung their song or proclaimed their message knowing that they were moving about in worlds not realized, clearly perceiving the incompleteness of the phenomenal world and the delusive nature of sense perceptions. They have known a Reality which they could not comprehend; felt a Presence which they could not grasp. They have found strength for the battle and peace for the pain by regarding nature as a dim projection, a tantalizing intimation of that other, conscious and creative life, that originating and directive force, which is not nature any more than the copper wire is the electric fluid which it carries—a force which was before it, which moves within it, which shall be after it.

So poet and believer and mystic find the key to nature, the interpretation of that alien and cruel world, not by sinking to its indifferent level, not by sentimental exaltation of its specious peace, its amoral cruelty and beauty, but by regarding it as the expression, the intimation rather, of a purposive Intelligence, a silent and infinite Force, beyond it all. So the pagan effuses over nature, gilding with his sentimentality the puddles that the beasts would cough at. And the scientist is interested in efficient causes, seeing nature as an unbroken sequence, an endless uniformity of cause and effect, against whose iron chain the spirit of mankind wages a foredoomed but never ending revolt. But the religionist, confessing the ruthless indifference, the amorality which he distrusts and fears, and not denying the majestic uniformity of order, nevertheless declares that these are not self-made, that the amorality is but one half and that the confusing half of the tale. The whole creation indeed groaneth and travaileth in pain, but for a final cause, which alone interprets or justifies it, and which eventually shall set it free. As a matter of fact, nearly all poets and artists thus view nature in the light of final causes, though often instinctively and unconsciously so. For what they sing or paint or mould is not the landscape that we see, the flesh we touch, but the life behind it, the light that never was on land or sea. What they give us is not a photograph or an inventory—it is worlds away from such naïve and lying realism. But they hint at the inexpressible behind expression; paint the beauty which is indistinguishable from nature but not identical with Nature. They make us see that not she, red in tooth and claw, but that intangible and supernal something-more, is what gives her the cleansing bath of loveliness. No reflective or imaginative person needs to be greatly troubled, therefore, by any purely mechanical or materialistic conception of the universe. They who would commend that view of the cosmos have not only to reckon with philosophical and religious idealism, but also with all the bright band of poets and artists and seers. Such an issue once resolutely forced would therewith collapse, for it would pit the qualitative standards against the quantitative, the imagination against literalism, the creative spirit in man against the machine in him.

Here, then, is the difference between the naturalist's and the religionist's attitude toward Nature. The believer judges Nature, well aware of the gulf between himself and her, hating with inexpressible depth of indignation and repudiating with profound contempt the sybarite's identification of human and natural law. But also he comes back to her, not to accept in wonder her variable outward form, but to worship in awe before her invariable inner meaning. Sometimes, like so many of the humanists, he rises only to a vague sense of the mystic unity that fills up the interspaces of the world, and cries with Wordsworth:

"... And I have felt

A presence that disturbs me with the joy

Of elevated thoughts; a sense sublime

Of something far more deeply interfused,

Whose dwelling is the light of setting suns,

And the round ocean and the living air,

And the blue sky, and in the mind of man;

A motion and a spirit, that impels

All thinking things, all objects of all thought,

And rolls through all things."[24]

Sometimes he dares to personalize this ultimate and then ascends to the supreme poetry of the religious experience and feels the cosmic consciousness, the eternal "I" of this strange world, which fills it with observant majesty. And then he chants,

"The heavens declare the glory of God,

The firmament showeth his handiwork."

Or he whispers,

"Whither shall I go from Thy spirit,

Or whither shall I flee from Thy presence?

If I ascend up into heaven, Thou art there,

If I make my bed in hell, behold Thou art there,

If I take the wings of the morning

And dwell in the uttermost parts of the earth,

Even there shall Thy hand lead me

And Thy right hand shall hold me."[25]

Indeed, the devout religionist almost never thinks of nature as such. She is always the bush which flames and is not consumed. Therefore he walks softly all his days, conscious that God is near.

"Of old," he says, "Thou hast laid the foundations of the earth;

And the heavens are the work of Thy hands.

They shall perish, but Thou shalt endure;

Yea, all of them shall wax old like a garment;

As a vesture shalt Thou change them, and they shall be changed;

But Thou art the same,

And Thy years shall have no end."[26]

To him nature is the glass through which he sees darkly and often with a darkling mind, the all-pervasive Presence; it is the veil—the veil that covers the face of God.

Here, then, we have the contrasting attitude of worldling and believer toward nature, the outward universe. Now we come to the contrasting attitude of humanist and believer toward man, the world within. For why are we so sure, first, of the chasm between ourselves and Nature and, second, that we can bridge that chasm by reaching out to something behind and beyond her which is more like us than her? What gives us the key to her dualism? Why do we think that there is Something which perpetually beckons to us through her, makes awful signs of an intimate and significant relationship? Because we feel a similar chasm, an equal cleft in our own hearts, a division in the moral nature of mankind. We know that gulf between us and the outward world because we know the greater gulf between flesh and spirit, between the natural man and the real man, between the "I" and the "other I."

Here is where the humanist bids us good-by and we must go forward on our road alone. For he will not acknowledge that there is anything essential or permanent in that divided inner world; he would minimize it or explain it away. But we know it is there and the reason we know there is Something without which can bridge the outer chasm is because we also know there is Something-Else within which might bridge this one. For we who are religious know that within the depths and the immensities of this inner world, where there is no space but where there is infinite largeness, where there is no time but where there is perpetual strife, there is Something-Else as well as the "I" and the "other I," and it is that He who is the Something-Else who alone can close the gap in that divided kingdom and make us one with ourselves, hence with Himself and hence with His world.

You ask how we can say, "He's there; He knows." We answer that this "other," this "He" is a constant figure in the experience; always in the vision; an integral part of the perception. What is He like? "He" is purity and compassion and inexorableness. Something fixed, immutable, not to be tricked, not to be evaded and oh! all-comprehending. He sees, his eyes run to and fro in all the dark and wide, the light and high dominions of the soul. If we will not come to terms with "Him," that eternal and changeless life will be the cliff against which the tumultuous waves of the divided spirit shall shatter and dissipate into soundless foam; if we will come to terms, relinquish, accept, surrender, then that purity and that compassion will be the cleansing tide, the healing and restoring flood in which we sink in the ecstasy of self-loss to arise refreshed, radiant, and made whole.

So we reckon from within out. The religious view of the world is based upon the religious experience of the soul. We have no other means of getting at reality. I know that there is Something-more than me and Something-more than the nature outside of me, because we know that there is Something which is not me and is not nature, inside of me. So the man of religion, like any other poet, artist, seer, looks in his own heart and writes. What he finds there is real, or else, as far as he is concerned, there is no reality. He does not assert that this reality is the final and utter truth. But he knows it is his trustworthy mediator of that truth.

Here, then, is an immense separation between religionist and both humanist and naturalist; a separation so complete as to come full circle. We are convinced of the secondary value, both of natural appearances and of the mortal, temporal consciousness. So we substitute for impertinent familiarity with Nature, a reverent regard for what she half reveals, half hides. We interpret her by ourselves. We are the same compound of identity and difference. We acknowledge our continuity with the natural world, our intimate and tragic alliance with the dust, but we also know that we, within ourselves, are Something-Else as well. And it is that Something-Else in us which makes the significant part of us, which sets our value and place in the scale of being.

In short, the dualism of nature is revealed in the dualism of the soul. There is a gulf within, and if only man can span the inner chasm, he will know how to bridge the outer. He must begin by finding God within himself, or he will never find Him anywhere. Now, it is out of this sense of a separation within himself, from himself and from the Author of himself, that there arises that awful sense of helplessness, of dependence, of bewilderment, which is the second great element in the religious life. Man is alone in the world; man is helpless in the world; man ought not to be alone in the world; man is therefore under scrutiny and condemnation; he must find reconciliation, harmony, companionship, somehow, somewhere. Hence the religious man is not arrogant like the pagan, nor proud like the humanist; he is humble. It is Burke, I think, who says that the whole ethical life of man has its roots in this humility.[27] The religious man cannot help but be humble. He has an awful pride in his kinship with heaven, but, standing before the Lord of heaven, he feels human nature's proper place, its confusion and division and helplessness; its dependence upon the higher Power.

It is at this point that humanism and religion definitely part company. The former does not feel this absolute and judging Presence, hence cannot understand the spiritual solicitude of the latter. St. Paul was not quite at home on Mars Hill; it was hard to make those who were always hearing and seeing some new thing understand; the shame and humility of the cross were an unnecessary foolishness to them. So they have always been. The humanist cannot take seriously this sense of a transcendent reality. When Cicero, to escape the vengeance of Clodius, withdrew from Rome, he passed over into Greece and dwelt for a while in Thessalonica. One day he saw Mount Olympus, the lofty and eternal home of the deities of ancient Greece. "But I," said the bland eclectic philosopher, "saw nothing but snow and ice."

How inadequate, then, as a substitute for religion, is even the noblest humanism. True and fine as far as it goes, it does not go far enough for us. It takes too little account of the divided life. It appears not to understand it. On the whole it refuses to acknowledge that it really exists, or, if it does, it is convinced of man's unaided ability to efface it. It isn't something inevitable. Hence the pride which is an essential quality of the humanistic attitude.

But the religious man knows that it does exist and that while he is not wholly responsible for it, yet he is essentially so and that, alas, in spite of that fact, he alone cannot bridge it. So he cries, "Wretched man that I am, what shall I do to be saved?" Here is the feeling of uneasiness, the sense of something being wrong about us as we naturally stand, of which James speaks. In that sense of responsibility is the confession of sin and in the confession of sin is the acknowledgment of the impotence of the sinner.

"The moving finger writes, and having writ, moves on

Nor all your wit nor all your tears, can wash a line of it."

Man cannot, unaided, make his connection with this higher power. The world is at fault, yes, but we are at fault, something both within and without dreadfully needs explaining. So man is subdued and troubled by the infinite mystery; and he cannot accept the place in which he finds himself in that mystery; he is ashamed of it.

Vivid, then, is his sense of helplessness! It makes him resent the humanist, who bids him, unaided, solve his fate and be a man. That is giving him stones when he asks for bread. He knows that advice makes an inhuman demand upon the will; it assumes a reasonableness, an insight and a moral power, which for him do not exist; it ignores or it denies the reality and the meaning of this inner gulf. It is important to note that even as philosophy and art and literature soon parted company with the naturalist, so, to a large degree, they part company with the humanist, too. They do not know very much of an harmonious and triumphant universe. Few of the world's creative spirits have ever denied that inner chasm or minimized its tragic consequences to mankind. Isaiah and Paul and John and Augustine and Luther are wrung with the consciousness of it. Indeed, the antithesis between flesh and spirit is too familiar in religious literature to need any recounting. It is more vividly brought home to us from the nonprofessional, the disinterested and involuntary testimony of secular writing. Was there ever such a cry of revolt on the part of the trapped spirit against the net and slough of natural values and natural desires as runs through the sonnets of William Shakespeare? We remember the 104th:

"Poor soul, the centre of my sinful earth,

Foiled by these rebel powers that thee array,

Why dost thou pine within, and suffer dearth,

Painting thine outward walls so costly gay?

Why so large cost, having so short a lease,

Dost thou upon thy fading mansion spend?

Shall worms, inheritors of this excess,

Eat up thy charge? Is this thy body's end?

Then soul, live thou upon thy servant's loss

And let that pine to aggravate thy store,

Buy terms divine in selling hours of dross

Within be fed, without be rich no more—"

Or turn to our contemporary poet, James Stephens:

"Good and bad are in my heart
But I cannot tell to you
For they never are apart
Which is the better of the two.

I am this: I am the other
And the devil is my brother
And my father he is God
And my mother is the sod,
Therefore I am safe, you see
Owing to my pedigree.

So I cherish love and hate
Like twin brothers in a nest
Lest I find when it's too late
That the other was the best."[28]

Here, then, we find the next thing which grows out of man's sense of separation both from nature and from his own best self. It is his moral judgment on himself as well as on the world outside, and that power to judge shows that he is greater than either. As Dr. Gordon says, "Every honest man lives under the shadow of his own rebuke." We can go far with the humanist in acknowledging the failures that are due to environment, to incompleteness, to ignorance; we do not forget the helpless multitude who sit in darkness and in the shadow of death; and we agree with the scientist that their helplessness foredooms them and that their fate cannot be laid to their charge. But we go far beyond where scientist and humanist stop. For we know that the deepest cause of human misery is not inheritance, is not environment, is not ignorance, is not incompleteness; it is the informed but the perverse human will. Just as unhappiness is the consciousness of the divided mind, so guilt is this sense of the deliberately divided will. Jonathan Swift knew that; on every yearly recurrence of the hour in which he came into the world, he cried lamentably, "Let the day perish wherein I was born."

The Lord Jesus knew it, too. His teaching, unlike that of Paul, does not throw into the foreground the divided will and its accompanying sense of sin and guilt. But he does not ignore it. He brought it out with infinite tenderness but inexorable clearness in the parables of the lost sheep, the lost coin and the lost boy. The sheep were but young and silly, they did not wish to be lost on the mountain-side; they knew no better; inexperience, ignorance were theirs, and for their sad estate they were not held responsible. For them the compassionate shepherd sought until he found them in the wilds, took them, involuntary burdens, on his heart, brought them back to safety and the fold. The coin had no native affinity with the dirt and grime of the careless woman's house. It was only a coin, attached to anklet or bracelet, having no power, no independence of its own; where it fell, there must it lie. So with the lives set by fate in the refuse and grime of our industrial civilization, the pure minted gold effectually concealed by the obscurity and filth around. For such lives, victims of environment, the Father will search, too, until they are found, taken up, and somewhere, in this world or another, restored to their native worth. But the chief of the parables, and the one that has captured the imagination and subdued the heart of mankind, because it so true to the greater part of life, is the story of the lost boy. For he was the real sinner and he was such because, knowing what he was about and able to choose, he desired to do wrong. It was not ignorance, nor environment, nor inheritance, that led him into the far country. It was its alien delights and their alien nature, for which as such he craved. How subtle and certain is the word of Jesus here. No shepherd seeks this wandering sheep; no householder searches for this lost coin. The boy who willed to do wrong must stay with the swine among the husks until he wills to do right. Then, when he desires to return, return is made possible and easy, but the responsibility is forever his. The source of his misery is his own will.

So the disposition of mankind is at the bottom of the suffering and the division. There is rebellion and perverseness mingled with the helplessness and ignorance and sorrow. No man ever understands or can speak to the religious life unless he has the consciousness of this inner moral cleft. No man will ever be able to preach with power about God unless he does it chiefly in terms of God's difference from man and man's perilous estate and desperate need of Him. Indeed, God is not like us, not like this inner life of ours; this is what we want to hear. God is different; that is why we want to be able to love Him. And being thus different, we are separated from Him, both by the inner chasm of the divided soul and the outer chasm of remote and hostile nature. Then comes the final question: How are we, being helpless, to reach Him? How are we, being guilty, to find Him?

When men deal with these queries, with this range of experience, this set of inward perceptions, then they are preaching religiously. And then, I venture to say, they do not fail either of hearers or of followers. Then there is what Catherine Booth used to call "liberty of speech"; then there is power because then we talk of realities. For what is it that looks out from the eyes of religious humanity? Rebellion, pride? no! Humility, loneliness, something of a just and deserved fear; but most of all, desire, insatiable, unwavering, an intense desire. This passion of the race, its never satisfied hunger, its incredible intensity and persistency of striving and longing, is at once the tragedy and glory, the witness to the helplessness, the revelation of the capacity of the race. The mainspring of human activity, the creative impulse from which in devious ways all the thousand-hued motives of our lives arise, is revealed in the ancient cry, "My soul thirsteth for God, for the living God!" That unquenched thirst for Him underlies all human life, as the solemn stillness of the ocean underlies the restless upper waves. The dynamic of the world is the sense of the divine reality. The woe of the world is man's inability to discover and appropriate that reality. Who that has entered truly into life does not perceive beneath all the glitter of its brilliance, the roar of its energy and achievement, the note of melancholy? The great undertone of life is solemn in its pathetic uniformity. The poets and prophets of the world have seized unerringly upon that melancholy undertone. Who ever better understood the futility and helplessness of unaided man, the certain doom that tracks down his pride of insolence, or his sin, than the Greek tragedians? Sophocles, divided spirit that he was, heard that note of melancholy long ago by the Ægean, wrote it into his somber dramas, with their turbid ebb and flow of human misery. Sometimes the voices of our humanity as they rise blend and compose into one great cry that is lifted, shivering and tingling, to the stars, "Oh, that I knew where I might find Him!" Sometimes and more often they sink into a subdued and minor plaint, infinitely touching in its human solicitude, perplexity and pain. Again, James Stephens has phrased it for us in his verse *The Nodding Stars*.[20]

"Brothers, what is it ye mean,

What is it ye try to say

That so earnestly ye lean

From the spirit to the clay.

"There are weary gulfs between

Here and sunny Paradise,

Brothers! What is it ye mean

That ye search with burning eyes,

"Down for me whose fire is clogged,

Clamped in sullen, earthy mould,

Battened down and fogged and bogged,

Where the clay is seven-fold."

Now we understand the tragic aspect of nature and of the human soul caught in this cosmic dualism without which corresponds to the ethical dualism within. This perception of the One behind the many in nature, of the thing-in-itself, as distinguished from the many expressions of that thing, is the chief theme for preaching. This is what brings men to themselves. Herein, as Dr. Newman Smyth has pointed out, appears the unique marvel of personality. "It becomes conscious of itself as individual and it individualizes the world; it is the one discovering itself among the many. In the midst of uniformities of nature, moving at will on the plane of natural necessities, weaving the pattern of its ideas through the warp of natural laws, runs the personal life. On the same plane and amid these uniformities, yet itself a sphere of being of another order; in it, yet disentangled from it, and having its center in itself, it lives and moves and has its being, breaking no thread of nature's weaving, subject to its own law, and manifesting a dynamic of its own."[30]

The source, then, as we see it, of all human hopes and human dignity, the urge that lies behind all metaphysics and much of literature and art, the thing that makes men eager to live, yet nobly curious to die, is this conviction that One like unto ourselves but from whom we have made ourselves unlike, akin to our real, if buried, person, walketh with us in the fiery furnace of our life. There is a Spirit in man and the breath of the Almighty giveth him understanding. Starting from this interpretation, we can begin to order the baffling and teasing aspects, the illusive nature of the world. Why this ever failing, but never ending struggle against unseen odds to grasp and understand and live with the Divine? Why, between the two, the absolute and the changeless spirit, unseen but felt, and the hesitant and timid spirit of a man, would there seem to be a great gulf fixed? Because we are wrong. Because man finds the gulf within himself. He chafes at the limitations of time and space? Yes; but he chafes more at the mystery and weakness, the mingled deceitfulness and cunning and splendor of the human heart. Because there is no one of us who can say, I have made my life pure, I am free from my sin. He knows that the gulf is there between the fallible and human, and the more than human; he does not know how to cross it; he says,

"I would think until I found

Something I can never find

Something lying on the ground

In the bottom of my mind."

Here, then, can we not understand that mingling of mystic dignity and profound humility, of awe-struck pride and utter self-abnegation, wherewith the man of religion regards his race and himself? He is the child of the Eternal; he, being man, alone knows that God is. "When I consider the heavens, the work of Thy fingers, the moon and the stars which Thou hast ordained, what is man that Thou art mindful of him, or the son of man that Thou visitest him?" Here is the humility: "Why so hot, little man!" Then comes the awe-struck pride: "Yet Thou hast made him a little lower than the angels and crowned him with glory and honor." "Alone with the gods, alone!" God is the high and lofty one which inhabiteth eternity, but He is also nigh unto them who are of a broken and a contrite heart.

Here we are come to the very heart of religion. Man's proud separateness in the universe; yet man's moral defection and his responsibility for it which makes him know that separateness; man's shame and helplessness under it. Over against the denial or evasion of moral values by the naturalist and the dullness to the sense of moral helplessness by the humanist, there stands the sense of moral difference, the sense of sin, of penitence and confession. No preaching not founded on these things can ever be called religious or can ever stir those ranges of the human life for which alone preaching is supposed to exist.

What is the religious law, then? It is the law of humility. And what is the religious consciousness? The sense of man's difference from nature and from God. The sense of his difference from himself within himself and the longing for an inner harmony which shall unite him with himself and with the beauty and the spirit without. So what is the religious passion? Is it to exalt human nature? It would be more true to say it is to lose it. What is the end for us? Not identification with nature and the natural self, but pursuit of the other than nature, the more than natural self. Our humility is not like that of Uriah Heep, a mean opinion of ourselves in comparison with other men. It is the profound consciousness of the weakness and the nothingness of our kind, and of the poor ends human nature sets its heart upon, in comparison with that Other One above and beyond and without us, to whom we are kin, from whom we are different, to whom we aspire, to reach whom we know not how.

This, then, is what we mean when we turn back from the language of experience to the vocabulary of philosophy and theology and talk about the absolute values of religion. We mean by "absolute values" that behind the multifarious and ever changing nature, is a single and a steadfast cause—a great rock in a weary land. We have lost the old absolute philosophies and dogmatic theologies and that is good and right, for they were outworn. But we are never going to lose the central experience that produced them, and our task is to find a new philosophy to express these inner things for which the words "supernatural," "absolute," are no longer intelligible. For we still know that behind man's partial and relative knowledge, feeling, willing, is an utter knowledge, a perfect feeling, a serene and unswerving will; that beneath man's moral anarchy there is moral sovereignty; that behind his helplessness there is abundant power to save. Perhaps this Other is always changing, but, if so, it is a Oneness which is changing. In short, the thing that is characteristic of religion is that it dwells, not on man's likenesses, but on his awful differences from nature and from God; sees him not as little counterparts of deity, but as broken fragments only to be made whole within the perfect life. It sees relativity as the law of our being, yes, but relativity, not of the sort that excludes, but is included in, a higher absolute, even as the planet swings in infinite space.

The trouble with much preaching is that it lacks the essentially religious insight; in dwelling on man's identities it confuses or drugs, not clarifies and purges, the spirit. Thus, it obscures the gulf. Sometimes it evades it, or bridges it by minimizing it, and genuinely religious people, and those who want to be religious, and those who might be, know that such preaching is not real and that it does not move them and, worst of all, the hungry sheep look up and are not fed. For in such preaching there is no call to humility, no plea for grace, no sense that the achievement of self-unity is as much a rescue as it is a reformation. But this sense of the need of salvation is integral to religion; this is where it has parted company with humanism. Humanism makes no organic relations between man and the Eternal. It is as though it thought these would take care of themselves! In the place of grace it puts pride; pride of caste, of family, of character, of intellect. But high self-discipline and pride in the human spirit are not the deepest or the highest notes man strikes. The cry, not of pride in self, but for fellowship with the Infinite, is the superlative expression of man. Augustine sounded the highest note of feeling when he wrote, "O God, Thou hast made us for Thyself, and our hearts are restless until they rest in Thee." The words of the Lord Jesus gave the clearest insight of the human mind when He said, "And when he came to himself, he said, I will arise and go to my Father."

Footnote 22: (return)

"Agnosticism," the *Nineteenth Century*, February, 1889.

Footnote 23: (return)

The Meaning of God in Human Experience, p. 236.

Footnote 24: (return)

Lines composed a few miles above Tintern Abbey, stanza 3, ll. 36-45.

Footnote 25: (return)

Psalm cxxxix. 7-9.

Footnote 26: (return)

Psalm cii. 25-27.

Footnote 27: (return)

Correspondence, III, p. 213.

Footnote 28: (return)

Songs from the Clay, p. 40.

Footnote 29: (return)

Songs from the Clay, p. 68.

Footnote 30: (return)

The Meaning of the Personal Life, p. 173.

CHAPTER FIVE
Grace, Knowledge, Virtue

I hope the concluding paragraphs of the last chapter brought us back into the atmosphere of religion, into that sort of mood in which the reality of the struggle for character, the craving of the human spirit to give and to receive compassion, the cry of the lonely soul for the love of God, were made manifest. These are the real goods of life to religious natures; they need this meat which the world knoweth not of; there is a continuing resolve in them to say, "Good-by, proud world, I'm going home!" The genuinely religious man must, and should indeed, live in this world, but he cannot live of it.

Merely to create such an atmosphere then, to induce this sort of mood, to shift for men their perspectives, until these needs and values rise once more compelling before their eyes, is a chief end of preaching. Its object is not so much moralizing or instructing as it is interpreting and revealing; not the plotting out of the landscape at our feet, but the lifting of our eyes to the hills, to the fixed stars. Then we really do see things that are large as large and things that are small as small. We need that vision today from religious leaders more than we need any other one thing.

For humanism and naturalism between them have brought us to an almost complete secularization of preaching, in which its characteristic elements, its distinctive contribution, have largely faded from liberal speaking and from the consciousness of its hearers. We have emphasized man's kinship with nature until now we can see him again declining to the brute; we have proclaimed the divine Immanence until we think to compass the Eternal within a facile and finite comprehension. By thus dwelling on the physical and rational elements of human experience, religion has come to concern itself to an extraordinary degree with the local and temporal reaches of faith. We have lost the sense of communion with Absolute Being and of the obligation to standards higher than those of the world, which that communion brings. Out of this identification of man with nature has come the preaching which ignores the fact of sin; which reduces free will and the moral responsibility of the individual to the vanishing point; which stresses the control of the forces of inheritance and environment to the edge of fatalistic determinism; which leads man to regard himself as unfortunate rather than reprehensible when moral disaster overtakes him; which induces that condoning of the moral rebel which is born not of love for the sinner but of indifference to his sin; which issues in that last degeneration of self-pity in which individuals and societies alike indulge; and in that repellent sentimentality over vice and crime which beflowers the murderer while it forgets its victim, which turns to ouija boards and levitated tables to obscure the solemn finality of death and to gloze over the guilty secrets of the battlefield.

Thus it has come about that we preach of God in terms of the drawing-room, as though he were some vast St. Nicholas, sitting up there in the sky or amiably informing our present world, regarding with easy benevolence His minute and multifarious creations, winking at our pride, our cruelty, our self-love, our lust, not greatly caring if we break His laws, tossing out His indiscriminate gifts, and vaguely trusting in our automatic arrival at virtue. Even as in philosophy, it is psychologists, experts in empirical science and methods, and sociologists, experts in practical ethics, who may be found, while the historian and the metaphysician are increasingly rare, so in preaching we are amiable and pious and ethical and practical and informative, but the vision and the absolutism of religion are a departing glory.

What complicates the danger and difficulty of such a position, with its confusion of natural and human values, and its rationalizing and secularizing of theistic thinking, is that it has its measure of reality. All these observations of naturalist and humanist are half truths, and for that very reason more perilous than utter falsehoods. For the mind tends to rest contented within their areas, and so the partial becomes the worst enemy of the whole. What we have been doing is stressing the indubitable identity between man and nature and between the Creator and His creatures to the point of unreality, forgetting the equally important fact of the difference, the distinction between the two. But sound knowledge and normal feeling rest upon observing and reckoning with both aspects of this law of kinship and contrast. All human experience becomes known to us through the interplay of what appear to be contradictory needs and opposing truths within our being. Thus, man is a social animal and can only find himself in a series of relationships as producer, lover, husband, father and friend. He is a part of and like unto his kind, his spirit immanent in his race. But man is also a solitary creature, and in that very solitariness, which he knows as he contrasts it with his social interests, he finds identity of self, the something which makes us "us," which separates us from all others in the world. A Crusoe, marooned on a South Sea island, without even a black man Friday for companionship, would soon cease to be a man; personality would forsake him. But the same Crusoe is equally in need of solitude. The hell of the barracks, no matter how well conducted, is their hideous lack of privacy; men condemned by shipwreck or imprisonment to an unbroken and intimate companionship kill their comrade or themselves. We are all alike and hence gregarious; we are all different and hence flee as a bird to the mountain. The reality of human personality lies in neither one aspect of the truth nor the other, but in both. The truth is found as we hold the balance between identity and difference. Hence we are not able to think of personality in the Godhead unless we conceive of God as being, within Himself, a social no less than a solitary Being.

Again, this law that the truth is found in the balance of the antinomies appears in man's equal passion for continuity and permanency and for variety and change. The book of Revelation tells us that the redeemed, before the great white throne, standing upon the sea of glass, sing the song of Moses and the Lamb. What has the one to do with the other? Here is the savage, triumphant chant of the far dawn of Israel's history, joined with the furthest and latest possible events and words. Well, it at least suggests the continuity of the ageless struggle of mankind, showing that the past has its place in the present, relieving man's horror of the impermanence, the disjointed character of existence. He wants something orderly and static. But, like the jet of water in the fountain, his life is forever collapsing and collapsing, falling in upon itself, its apparent permanence nothing but a rapid and glittering succession of impermanences. The dread of growing old is chiefly that, as years come on, life changes more and faster, becomes a continual process of readjustment. Therefore we want something fixed; like the sailor with his compass, we must have some needle, even if a tremulous one, always pointing toward a changeless star. Yet this is but one half of the picture. Does man desire continuity?—quite as much does he wish for variety, cessation of old ways, change and fresh beginnings. The most terrible figure which the subtle imagination of the Middle Ages conjured up was that of the Wandering Jew, the man who could not die! Here, then, we arrive at knowledge, the genuine values of experience, by this same balancing of opposites. Continuity alone kills; perpetual change strips life of significance; man must have both.

Now, it is in the religious field that this interests us most. We have seen that what we have been doing there of late has been to ignore the fact that reality is found only through this balancing of the law of difference and identity, contrast and likeness. We have been absorbed in one half of reality, identifying man with nature, prating of his self-sufficiency, seeing divinity almost exclusively as immanent in the phenomenal world. Thus we have not merely been dealing with only one half of the truth, but that, to use a solecism, the lesser half.

For doubtless men do desire in religion a recognition of the real values of their physical nature. And they want rules of conduct, a guide for practical affairs, a scale of values for this world. This satisfies the craving for temporal adjustment, the sense of the goodness and worth of what our instinct transmits to us. But it does nothing to meet that profound dissatisfaction with this world and that sense of the encumbrances of the flesh which is also a part of reality and, to the religious man, perhaps the greater part. He wants to turn away from all these present things and be kept secretly in a pavilion from the strife of tongues. Here he has no continuing city. Always while we dwell here we have a dim and restless sense that we are in an unreal country and we know, in our still moments, that we shall only come to ourselves when we return to the house of our Father. Hence men have never been satisfied with religious leaders who chiefly interpreted this world to them.

And indeed, since July, 1914, and down to and including this very hour, this idealizing of time, which we had almost accepted as our office, has had a ghastly exposure. Because there has come upon us all one of these irrevocable and irremediable disasters, for which time has no word of hope, to which Nature is totally indifferent, for which the God of the outgoings and incomings of the morning is too small. For millions of living and suffering men and women all temporal and mortal values have been wiped out. They have been caught in a catastrophe so ruthless and dreadful that it has strewed their bodies in heaps over the fields and valleys of many nations. Today central and south and northeastern Europe and western Asia are filled with idle and hungry and desperate men and women. They have been deprived of peace, of security, of bread, of enlightenment alike. Something more than temporal salvation and human words of hope are needed here. Something more than ethical reform and social readjustment and economic alleviation, admirable though these are! Something there must be in human nature that eclipses human nature, if it is to endure so much! What has the God of this world to give for youth, deprived of their physical immortality and all their sweet and inalienable human rights, who are lying now beneath the acre upon acre of tottering wooden crosses in their soldier's graves? Is there anything in this world sufficient now for the widow, the orphan, the cripple, the starving, the disillusioned and the desperate? What Europe wants to know is why and for what purpose this holocaust—is there anything beyond, was there anything before it? A civilization dedicated to speed and power and utility and mere intelligence cannot answer these questions. Neither can a religion resolved into naught but the ethics of Jesus answer them. "If in this world only," cries today the voice of our humanity, "we have hope, then we are of all men the most miserable!" When one sees our American society of this moment returning so easily to the physical and the obvious and the practical things of life; when one sees the church immersed in programs, and moralizing, and hospitals, and campaigns, and membership drives, and statistics, and money getting, one is constrained to ask, "What shall be said of the human spirit that it can forget so soon?"

Is it not obvious, then, that our task for a pagan society and a self-contained humanity is to restore the balance of the religious consciousness and to dwell, not on man's identity with Nature, but on his far-flung difference; not on his self-sufficiency, but on his tragic helplessness; not on the God of the market place, the office and the street, an immanent and relative deity, but on the Absolute, that high and lofty One who inhabiteth eternity? Indeed, we are being solemnly reminded today that the other-worldliness of religion, its concern with future, supertemporal things, is its characteristic and most precious contribution to the world. We are seeing how every human problem when pressed to its ultimate issue becomes theological. Here is where the fertile field for contemporary preaching lies. It is found, not in remaining with those elements in the religious consciousness which it shares in common with naturalism and humanism, but in passing over to those which are distinctive to itself alone. It has always been true, but it is especially true at this moment, that effective preaching has to do chiefly with transcendent values.

Our task is to assert, first, then, the "otherness" of man, his difference from Nature, to point out the illusoriness of her phenomena for him, the derived reality and secondary value of her facts. These are things that need religious elucidation. The phrase "other-worldliness" has come, not without reason, to have an evil connotation among us, but there is nevertheless a genuine disdain of this world, a sense of high superiority to it and profound indifference toward it, which is of the essence of the religious attitude. He who knows that here he is a stranger, sojourning in tabernacles; that he belongs by his nature, not to this world, but that he seeks a better, that is to say, a heavenly country, will for the joy that is set before him, endure a cross and will despise the shame. He will have a conscious superiority to hostile facts of whatever sort or magnitude, for he knows that they deceive in so far as they pretend to finality. When religion has thus acquired a clear-sighted and thoroughgoing indifference to the natural order, then, and then only, it begins to be potent within that order. Then, as Professor Hocking says, it rises superior to the world of facts and becomes irresistible.[31]

The time is ripe, then, first, for the preacher to emphasize the inward and essential difference between man and nature which exists under the outward likeness, to remind him of this more-than-nature, this "otherness" of man, without which he would lose his most precious possession, the sense of personality. Faith begins by recognizing this transcendent element in man and the acceptance of it is the foundation of religious preaching. What was the worst thing about the war? Not its destruction nor its horrors nor its futilities, but its shames; the dreadful indignities which it inflicted upon man; it treated men as though they were not souls! No such moral catastrophe could have overwhelmed us if we had not for long let the brute lie too near the values and practices of our lives, depersonalizing thus, in politics and industry and morals and religion, our civilization. It all proceeded from the irreligious interpretation of human existence, and the fruits of that interpretation are before us.

The first task of the preacher, then, is to combat the naturalistic interpretation of humanity with every insight and every conviction that is within his power. If we are to restore religious values, rebuild a world of transcendent ends and more-than-natural beauty, we must begin here with man. In the popular understanding of the phrase all life is not essentially one in kind; physical self-preservation and reproduction are not the be-all and the end-all of existence. There is something more to be expressed in man without which these are but dust and ashes in the mouth. There is another kind of life mixed in with this, the obvious. If we cannot express the other world, we shall not long tolerate this one. To think that this world is all, leans toward madness; such a picture of man is a travesty, not a portrait of his nature. Only on some such basic truths as these can we build character in our young people. Paganism tells them that it is neither natural nor possible to keep themselves unspotted from the world. Over against it we must reiterate, You can and you must! for the man that sinneth wrongeth his own soul. You are something more than physical hunger and reproductive instinct; you are of spirit no less than dust. How, then, can you do this great sin against God!

How abundant here are the data with which religious preaching may deal. Indeed, as Huxley and scores of others have pointed out, it is only the religious view of man that builds up civilization. A great community is the record of man's supernaturalism, his uniqueness. It is built on the "higher-than-self" principle which is involved in the moral sense itself. And this higher-than-self is not just a collective naturalism, a social consciousness, as Durkheim and Overstreet and Miss Harrison would say. The simplest introspective act will prove that. For a man cannot ignore self-condemnation as if it were only a natural difficulty, nor disparage it as though it were merely humanly imposed. We think it comes from that which is above and without, because it speaks to the solitary and the unique, not the social and the common part of us. Hence conscience is not chiefly a tribal product, for it is what separates us from the group and in our isolation unites us with something other than the group. "Against Thee, Thee only, have I sinned and done this evil in Thy sight." So religious preaching perpetually holds us up above our natural selves and the natural order.

Thus man must live by an other-than-natural law if he is to preserve the family, which is the social unit of civilization. Its very existence depends upon modifying and transforming natural hunger by a diviner instinct, by making voluntary repressions, willing sacrifices of the lower to the higher, the subordinating of the law of self and might to the law of sacrifice and love—this is what preserves family life. Animals indeed rear and cherish their young and for the mating season remain true to one another, but no animality *per se* ever yet built a home. There must be a more-than-natural law in the state. Our national life and honor rest upon the stability of the democracy and we can only maintain that by walking a very straight and narrow path. For the peace of freedom as distinguished from precarious license is a more-than-natural attainment, born of self-repression and social discipline, the voluntary relinquishment of lesser rights for higher rights, of personal privileges for the sake of the common good. Government by the broad and easy path, following the lines of least resistance, like the natural order, saying might is right, means either tyranny or anarchy. *Circumspice*! One of the glories of western civilization is its hospitals. They stand for the supernatural doctrine of the survival of the unfit, the conviction of the community that, to take the easy path of casting out the aged and infirm, the sick and the suffering, would mean incalculable degeneration of national character, and that the difficult and costly path of protection and ministering service is both necessary and right. And why is the reformatory replacing the prison? Because we have learned that the obvious, natural way of dealing with the criminal certainly destroys him and threatens to destroy us; and that the hard, difficult path of reeducating and reforming a vicious life is the one which the state for her own safety must follow.

Genuine preaching, then, first of all, calls men to repentance, bids them turn away from their natural selves, and, to find that other and realer self, enter the straight and narrow gate. The call is not an arbitrary command, born of a negative and repressive spirit. It is a profound exhortation based upon a fundamental law of human progress, having behind it the inviolable sanction of the truth. Such preaching would have the authentic note. It is self-verifying. It stirs to answer that quality—both moral and imaginative—in the spirit of man which craves the pain and difficulty and satisfaction of separation from the natural order. It appeals to a timeless worth in man which transcends any values of mere intelligence which vary with the ages, or any material prosperity which perishes with the using, or any volitional activity that dies in its own expenditure. Much of the philosophy of Socrates was long ago outmoded, but Socrates himself, as depicted in the Phaedo, confronting death with the cup of hemlock in his hand, saying with a smile, "There is no evil which can happen to a good man living or dead," has a more-than-natural, an enduring and transcendent quality. Whenever we preach to the element in mankind which produces such attitudes toward life and bid it assert itself, then we are doing religious preaching, and then we speak with power. Jesus lived within the inexorable circle of the ideas of His time; He staked much on the coming of the new kingdom which did not appear either when or as He had first expected it. He had to adjust, as do we all, His life to His experience, His destiny to His fate. But when He was hanging on His cross, forgotten of men and apparently deserted by His God, something in Him that had nothing to do with nature or the brute rose to a final expression and by its more-than-natural reality, sealed and authenticated His life. Looking down upon His torturers, understanding them far better than they understood themselves, He cried, "Father, forgive them, for they know not what they do." That cry has no place in nature; it has no application and no meaning outside the human heart and that which is above, not beneath, the human heart, from which it is derived. There, then, again was the supernatural law; there was the more-than-nature in man which makes nature into human nature; and there is the thing to whose discovery, cultivation, expression, real preaching is addressed. Every time a man truly preaches he so portrays what men ought to be, must be, and can be if they will, that they know there is something here

"that leaps life's narrow bars

To claim its birthright with the hosts of heaven!

A seed of sunshine that doth leaven

Our earthly dullness with the beams of stars,

And glorify our clay

With light from fountains elder than the Day."[32]

Such preaching is a perpetual refutation of and rebuke to the naturalism and imperialism of our present society. It is the call to the absolute in man, to a clear issue with evil. It would not cry peace, peace, when there is no peace. It would be living and active, and sharper than any two-edged sword, piercing even to the dividing of both joints and marrow, quick to discern the thoughts and intents of the heart.

Following this insistence upon the difference from nature, the more-than-natural in man, the second thing in religious preaching will have to be, obviously, the message of salvation. That is to say, reducing the statement to its lowest terms, if man is to live by such a law, the law of more-than-nature, then he must have something also more-than-human to help him in his task. He will need strength from outside. Indeed, because religion declares that there is such divine assistance, and that faith can command it, is the chief cause and reason for our existence. When we cease to preach salvation in some form or other, we deny our own selves; we efface our own existence. For no one can preach the more-than-human in mankind without emphasizing those elements of free will, moral responsibility, the need and capacity for struggle and holiness in human life which it indicates, and which in every age have been a part of the message of Him who said, "Be ye therefore perfect, even as your Father, which is in heaven, is perfect."

Therefore, as we have previously corrected the half truth of the naturalist who makes a caricature, not a portrait of man, we must now in the same way turn to the correcting of the humanist's emphasis upon man's native capacity and insist upon the complementary truth which fulfills this moral heroism of mankind, namely, the divine rescue which answers to its inadequacy. Man must struggle for his victory; he can win; he cannot win alone. We must then insist upon the doctrine of salvation, turning ourselves to the other side of the humanist's picture. Man cannot live by this more-than-natural law unaided. For not only has he the power to rise above Nature; the same thing gives him equal capacity to sink beneath her, and, when left to himself, he generally does so. The preacher does not dare deny the sovereignty of sin. Humanism hates the very name of sin; it has never made any serious attempt to explain the consciousness of guilt. Neither naturalist nor humanist can afford to admit sin, for sin takes man, as holiness does, outside the iron chain of cause and effect; it breaks the law; it is not strictly natural. It makes clear enough that man is outside the natural order in two ways. He is both inferior and superior to it. He falls beneath, he rises above it. When he acts like a beast, he is not clean and beastly, but unclean and bestial. When he lifts his head in moral anguish, bathes all his spirit in the flood of awe and repentance, is transfigured with the glorious madness of self-sacrifice, he is so many worlds higher than the beast that their relationship becomes irrelevant. So we must deal more completely than humanists do with the central mystery of our experience; man's impotent idealism, his insight not matched with consummation; the fact that what he dares to dream of he is not able alone to do.

For the humanist exalts man, which is good; but then he makes him self-sufficient for the struggle which such exaltation demands, which is bad. In that partial understanding he departs from truth. And what is it that makes the futility of so much present preaching? It is the acceptance of this doctrine of man's moral adequacy and consequently the almost total lack either of the assurance of grace or of the appeal to the will. No wonder such exhortations cannot stem the tide of an ever increasing worldliness. Such preaching stimulates the mind; in both the better and the worse preachers, it moves the emotions but it gives men little power to act on what they hear and feel to the transformation of their daily existence. Thus the humanistic sense of man's sufficiency, coupled with the inherent distrust of any notion of help from beyond and above, any belief in a reinforcing power which a critical rationalism cannot dissect and explain, has gradually ruled out of court the doctrine of salvation until the preacher's power, both to experience and to transmit it, has atrophied through disuse.

Who can doubt that one large reason why crude and indefensible concepts of the Christian faith have such a disconcerting vitality today is because they carry, in their outmoded, unethical, discredited forms, the truth of man's insufficiency in himself and the confident assurance of that something coming from without which will abundantly complete the struggling life within? They offer the assurance of that peace and moral victory which man so ardently desires, because they declare that it is both a discovery and a revelation, an achievement and a rescue. There are vigorous and rapidly growing popular movements of the day which rest their summation of faith on the quadrilateral of an inerrant and verbally inspired Scripture, the full deity of Jesus Christ, the efficacy of His substitutionary atonement, the speedy second coming of the Lord. No sane person can suppose that these cults succeed because of the ethical insight, the spiritual sensitiveness, the intellectual integrity of such a message. It does not possess these things. They succeed, in spite of their obscurantism, because they do confess and meet man's central need, his need to be saved. The power of that fact is what is able to carry so narrow and so indefensible a doctrine.

So the second problem of the preacher is clear. Man asserts his potential independence of the natural law. But to realize that, he must bridge the gulf between himself and the supernatural lawgiver to whose dictates he confesses he is subject. He is not free from the bondage of the lower, except through the bondage to the higher. Nor can he live by that higher law unaided and alone. Here we strike at the root of humanism. Its kindly tolerance of the church is built up on the proud conviction that we, with our distinctive doctrine of salvation, are superfluous, hence sometimes disingenuous and always negligible. The humanist believes that understanding takes the place of faith. What men need is not to be redeemed from their sins, but to be educated out of their follies.

But does right knowing in itself suffice to insure right doing? Socrates and Plato, with their indentification of knowledge and virtue, would appear to think so; the church has gone a long way, under humanistic pressure, in tacit acquiescence with their doctrine. Yet most of us, judging alike from internal and personal evidence and from external and social observation, would say that there was no sadder or more universal experience than that of the failure of right knowledge to secure right performance. Right knowledge is not in itself right living. We have striking testimony on that point from one of the greatest of all humanists, no less a person than

Confucius. "At seventy," he says, "I could follow what my heart desired without transgressing the law of measure."[33] The implication of such testimony makes no very good humanistic apologetic! Most of us, when desire has failed, can manage to attain, unaided, the identification of understanding and conduct, can climb to the poor heights of a worn-out and withered continence. But one wonders a little whether, then, the climbing seems to be worth while.

But the doctrine usually begins by minimizing the free agency of the individual, playing up the factors of compulsion, either of circumstance or inheritance or of ignorance, as being in themselves chiefly responsible for blameful acts. These are therefore considered involuntary and certain to be reformed when man knows better and has the corresponding strength of his knowledge. But Aristotle, who deals with this Socratic doctrine in the third book of the *Ethics*, very sensibly remarks, "It is ridiculous to lay the blame of our wrong actions upon external causes rather than upon the facility with which we ourselves are caught by such causes, and, while we take credit for our noble actions to ourselves, lay the blame of our shameful actions upon pleasure."[34] "The facility with which we are caught"—there is the religious understanding there is that perversion of will which conspires with the perils and chances of the world so that together they may undo the soul.

Of course, as Aristotle admits, there is this half truth lying at the root of the Socratic identification of virtue and knowledge that every vicious person is ignorant of what he ought to do and what he ought to abstain from doing in the sense that what he is about to do could not be defended upon any ground of enlightened self-interest. And so, while he finds sin sweet and evil pleasant, these are delusive experiences, which, if he saw life steadily and whole, he would know as such. But one reason for this ignorance is unwillingness to know. Good men do evil, and understanding men sin, partly because they are misled by false ideas, partly, also, because, knowing them false, they cannot or will not give them up. This is what Goethe very well understood when he said, "Most men prefer error to truth, because truth imposes limitations and error does not."

And another reason is that when men do know, they find a deadly and mysterious, a sort of perverted joy—a sweet and terrible and secret delight,—in denying their own understanding. Thus right living calls for a repeated and difficult exercise of the will, what Professor Babbitt calls "a pulling back of the impulse to the track that knowledge indicates." Such moral mastery is not identical with moral perception and most frequently is not its accompaniment, unless observation and experience are alike fallacious. Thus the whole argument falls to the ground when we confess that possession of knowledge does not guarantee the application of it.

Therefore the two things, knowledge and virtue, according to universal experience, are not identical. Humanists indeed use the word "knowledge" for the most part in an esoteric sense. Knowledge is virtue in the sense that it enables us to see virtue as excellent and desirable; it is not virtue in the sense that it alone enables us to acquire it.

Who, indeed, that has ever lived in the far country does not know that one factor in its fascination was a bittersweet awareness of the folly, the inevitable disaster, of such alien surroundings. Who also does not know that often when the whole will is set to identify conduct with conviction, it may be, for all its passionate and bitter sincerity, set in vain. In every hour of every day there are hundreds of lives that battle honestly, but with decreasing spiritual forces, with passion and temptation. Sometimes a life is driven by the fierce gales of enticement, the swift currents of desire, right upon the jagged rock of some great sin. Lives that have seemed strong and fair go down every day, do they not, and shock us for a moment with their irremediable catastrophe? And we must not forget that before they went down, for many a month or even year they have been hard beset lives. Before that final and complete ruin, they have been drifting and struggling, driven and fighting, sin drawing nearer and nearer, their fated lives urged on, the mind growing darker, the stars in their souls going out, the steering of their own lives taken from their hands. Then there has been the sense of the coming danger, the dark presentiment of how it all must end when the "powers that tend the soul to help it from the death that cannot die, and save it even in extremes, begin to vex and plague it." There has been the dreadful sense of life drifting toward a great crash, nearer and nearer to what must be the wreck of all things. What does the humanist have to offer to these men and women who know perfectly well where they are, and what they are about, and where they would like to be, but who can't get there and who are, today and every day, putting forth their last and somber efforts, trying in vain to just keep clear of ruin until the darkness and the helplessness shall lift and something or someone shall give them peace!

Now, it is this defect in the will which automatically limits the power of the intellect. It is this which the Socratic identification ignores. So while we might readily grant that it is in the essential nature of things that virtue and truth, wisdom and character, understanding and goodness, are but two aspects of one thing, is it not trifling with one of the most serious facts of human destiny to interpret the truism to mean that, when a man knows that a contemplated act is wrong or foolish or ugly, he is thereby restrained from accomplishing it? Knowledge is not virtue in the sense that mere reason or mere perception can control the will. And this is the conclusion that Aristotle also comes to when he says: "Some people say that incontinence is impossible, if one has knowledge. It seems to them strange, as it did to Socrates, that where knowledge exists in man, something else should master it and drag it about like a slave. Socrates was wholly opposed to this idea; he denied the existence of incontinence, arguing that nobody with a conception of what was best could act against it, and therefore, if he did so act, his action must be due to ignorance." And then Aristotle adds, "The theory is evidently at variance with the facts of experience."[35] Plato himself exposes the theoretical nature of the assertion, its inhuman demand upon the will, the superreasonableness which it expects but offers no way of obtaining, when he says, "Every one will admit that a nature having in perfection all the qualities which are required in a philosopher is a rare plant seldom seen among men."[36]

It would be well if those people who are going about the world today teaching social hygiene to adolescents (on the whole an admirable thing to do) but proceeding on the assumption that when youth knows what is right and what is wrong, and why it is right and why it is wrong, and what are the consequences of right and wrong, that then, *ipso facto*, youth will become chaste,—well if they would acquaint themselves either with the ethics of Aristotle or with the Christian doctrine of salvation. For if men think that knowledge by itself ever yet produced virtue in eager and unsated lives, they are either knaves or fools. They will find that knowledge uncontrolled by a purified spirit and a reinforced will is already teaching men not how to be good, but how to sin the more boldly with the better chance of physical impunity. "Philosophy," says Black, "is a feeble antagonist before passion, because it does not supply an adequate motive for the conflict."[37] There were few men in the nineteenth century in whom knowledge and virtue were more profoundly and completely joined than in John Henry Newman. But did that subtle intellect suffice? could it make the scholar into the saint? Hear his own words:

"O Holy Lord, who with the children three

    Didst walk the piercing flame;

Help, in those trial hours which, save to Thee,

    I dare not name;

Nor let these quivering eyes and sickening heart

    Crumble to dust beneath the tempter's dart.

"Thou who didst once Thy life from Mary's breast

    Renew from day to day;

O might her smile, severely sweet, but rest

On this frail clay!

Till I am Thine with my whole soul, and fear

Not feel, a secret joy, that Hell is near."

So, only when we include in the term "knowledge" understanding plus good will, is the humanist position true, and this, I suppose, is what Aristotle meant when he finally says, "Vice is consistent with knowledge of some kind, but it excludes knowledge in the full and proper sense of the word."[38]

Now, so finespun a discussion of intricate and psychological subtleties is mildly interesting presumably to middle-aged scholars, but I submit that a half truth that needs so much explanation and so many admissions before it can be made safe or actual, is a rather dangerous thing to offer to adolescence or to a congregation of average men and women. It cannot sound to them very much like the good news of Jesus. Culture is a precious thing, but no culture, without the help of divine grace and the responsive affection on our part which that grace induces, will ever knit men together in a kingdom of God, a spiritual society. As long ago as the second century Celsus understood that. He says in his polemic against Christianity, as quoted by Origen, "If any one suppose that it is possible that the people of Asia and Europe and Africa, Greeks and barbarians, should agree to follow one law, he is hopelessly ignorant."[39] Now, Celsus was proceeding on the assumption that Christianity was only another philosophy, a new intellectual system, and he was merely exposing the futility of all such unaided intellectualism.

It is, therefore, of prime importance for the preacher to remember that humanism, or any other doctrine which approaches the problem of life and conduct other than by moral and spiritual means, can never take the place of the religious appeal, because it does not touch the springs of action where motives are born and from which convictions arise. You do not make a man moral by enlightening him; it is nearer the truth to say that you enlighten him when you make him moral. "Blessed are the pure in heart," said Jesus, "for they shall see God. If any man wills to do the will, he shall know the doctrine." Education does not wipe out crime nor an understanding mind make a holy will. The last half of the nineteenth century made it terribly clear that the learning and science of mankind, where they are divorced from piety, unconsecrated by a spiritual passion, and largely directed by selfish motives, can neither benefit nor redeem the race. Consider for a moment the enormous expansion of knowledge which the world has witnessed since the year 1859. What prodigious accessions to the sum of our common understanding have we seen in the natural and the humane sciences; and what marvelous uses of scientific knowledge for practical purposes have we discovered! We have mastered in these latter days a thousand secrets of nature. We have freed the mind from old ignorance and ancient superstition. We have penetrated the secrets of the body, and can almost conquer death and indefinitely prolong the span of human days. We face the facts and know the world as our fathers could never do. We understand the past and foresee the future. But the most significant thing about our present situation is this: how little has this wisdom, in and of itself, done for us! It has made men more cunning rather than more noble. Still the body is ravaged and consumed by passion. Still men toil for others against their will, and the strong spill the blood of the weak for their ambition and the sweat of the children for their greed. Never was learning so diffused nor the content of scholarship so large as now. Yet the great cities are as Babylon and Rome of old, where human wreckage multiplies, and hideous vices flourish, and men toil without expectancy, and live without hope, and millions exist—not live at all—from hand to mouth. As we survey the universal unrest of the world today and see the horrors of war between nation and nation, and between class and class, it would not be difficult to make out a case for the thesis that the scientific and intellectual advances of the nineteenth century have largely worked to make men keener and more capacious in their suffering. And at least this is true; just so far as the achievement of the mind has been divorced from the consecration of the spirit, in just so far knowledge has had no beneficent potency for the human race.

Is it not clear, then, that preaching must deal again, never more indeed than now, with the religion which offers a redemption from sin? This is still foolishness to the Greeks, but to those who believe it is still the power of God unto salvation. Culture is not religion. When the preacher substitutes the one for the other, he gives stones for bread, and the hungry sheep go elsewhere or are not fed. It is this emasculated preaching, mulcted of its spiritual forces, which awakes the bitterest distrust and deepest indignation that human beings know. They are fighting the foes of the flesh and the enemies of the spirit, enduring the slings and arrows of outrageous fortune, standing by the open graves of their friends and kindred, saying there, "I shall go to him, but he shall not return to me." And then, with all this mystery and oppression of life upon them they enter the doors of the house of God and listen to a polite essay, are told of the consolations of art, reminded of the stupidity of evil, assured of the unreality of sin, offered the subtle satisfactions of a cultivated intelligence. In just so far as they are genuine men and women, they resent such preaching as an insult, a mockery and an offense. No, no; something more is needed than the humanist can offer for those who are hard-pressed participants in the stricken fields of life.

Religious preaching, then, begins with these two things: man's solitary place in nature, man's inability to hold that place alone. Hence two more things are necessary as essentials of great preaching in a pagan day. The clear proclamation of the superhuman God, the transcendent spirit who is able to control and reinforce the spirit of man, and the setting forth of some way or some mediator, through whom man may meet and touch that Spirit so far removed yet so infinitely near and dear to him. It is with these matters that we shall be occupied in the next chapter.

Footnote 31: (return)

The Meaning of God in Human Experience, p. 518.

Footnote 32: (return)

J.R. Lowell, *Commemoration Ode*, stanza IV, ll. 30-35.

Footnote 33: (return)

Analects, II, civ.

Footnote 34: (return)

Ethics, Book III, ch. ii, p. 61.

Footnote 35: (return)

Ethics, Book VII, ch. iii, pp. 206-207.

Footnote 36: (return)

Republic, VI, 491.

Footnote 37: (return)

Culture and Restraint, p. 104.

Footnote 38: (return)

Ethics, Book VII, ch. v, p. 215.

Footnote 39: (return)

Origen, contra Celsum, VIII, p. 72.

CHAPTER SIX
The Almighty and Everlasting God

If the transcendent element in man which endows him with the proud if tragic sense of personality is the first message of the preacher to a chattering and volatile world, and the second is the setting forth of what this endowment demands and how pitiably man fails to meet it, then the third message is of the Rock that is higher than he, even inclusive of his all, in whose composed and comprehensive Being his baffled and divided person may be gathered up, brought to its own consummation of self. The rivers that pour tumultuously to their ocean bed, the ascending fire ever falling backward but leaping upward to the sun, are poor figures to express the depth and irresistible urge of the passion in man for completeness, for repose, for power, for self-perception in self-expression, for victory and the attainment of the end. Conscious and divided spirit that he is, man turns away, sooner or later, with utter weariness and self-disgust from the nature which pleases him by betraying him, which maims his person that he may enjoy his senses, and reaches out after the other-worldly, the supernatural, the invisible and eternal Hope and Home of the Soul.

Humanism which bids men sufficiently find God within themselves, if they think they need to find Him at all, seems not to comprehend this passion of pride and humility, this inner perception of the futility and the blunder of the self-contained life. Life is so obviously not worth its brevity, its suffering, its withheld conclusions, its relative insignificance, if it must thus stand alone. All that can save it, preserve to it worth and dignity, maintain its self-respect and mastery, is to find that abundant power without which confesses, certifies and seals the divinity within.

How foredoomed to failure, then, especially in an age when men are surmounting life by placating it, enjoying it by being easy with themselves—how foredoomed to failure is the preaching which continues in the world of religion this exaltation of human sufficiency and natural values, domesticating them within the church. It is to laugh to see them there! It means so transparent a surrender, so pitiable a confession of defeat. If anything can bring the natural man into the sanctuary it is that there he has to bring his naturalness to the bar of a more-than-natural standard. If he comes at all, it will not be for entertainment and expansion but because there we insist on reverence and restraint. If church and preacher offer only a pietized and decorous naturalism, when he can get the real thing in naked and unashamed brutality without; if they offer him only another form of humanistic living, he will stay away. Such preaching is as boresome as it is unnecessary. Such exercise of devotion is essentially superfluous and a rather humorous imposition upon the world. The only thing that will ever bring the natural man to listen to preaching is when it insists upon something more-than-the-natural and calls him to account regarding it; when it speaks of something different and better for him than this world and what it can offer. "Take my *yoke* upon you" is the attractive invitation, "make inner obeisance and outward obedience to something higher than thy poor self."

It is clear, then, that these observations have a bearing upon our preaching of the doctrine of God. There is a certain illogicality, something humorous, in going into a church, of all places in the world, to be told how like we are to Him. The dull and average personality, the ordinary and not very valuable man, can probably listen indifferently and with a slow-growing hardness and dim resentment to that sort of preaching for a number of years. But the valuable, the highly personalized people, the saints and the sinners, the great rebels and the great disciples, who are the very folk for whom the church exists, would hate it, and they would know the final bitterness of despair if they thought that this was so. Either saint or sinner would consider it the supreme insult, the last pitch of insolence, for the church to be telling them that it is true.

For they know within themselves that it is a lie. Their one hope hangs on God because His thoughts are not their thoughts, nor His ways their ways; because He seeth the end from the beginning; because in Him there is no variableness, neither shadow that is caused by turning; because no man shall see His face and live. They, the sinners and the saints, do not want to be told that they, within themselves, can heal themselves and that sin has no real sinfulness. That is tempting them to the final denial, the last depth of betrayal, the blurring of moral values, the calling of evil good and the saying that good is evil. They know that this is the unpardonable madness. In the hours when they, the saints and sinners, wipe their mouths and say, "We have done no harm"; in the days when what they love is ugliness because it is ugly and shameless, and reckless expression because it is so terrible, so secretly appalling, so bittersweet with the sweetness of death, they know that it is the last affront to have the church—the one place where men expect they will be made to face the facts—bow these facts out of doors.

No, we readily grant that the religious approach to the whole truth and to final reality is like any other one, either scientific, economic, political, a partial approach. It sets forth for the most part only a group of facts. When it does not emphasize other facts, it does not thereby deny them. But it insists that the truth of man's differences, man's helplessness which the differences reveal, and man's fate hanging therefore upon a transcendent

God, are the key truths for the religious life. It is with that aspect of life the preacher deals, and if he fails to grapple with these problems and considerations, ignores these facts, his candlestick has been removed.

The argument for a God, then, within His world, but also distinct from it, above its evil custom and in some sense untouched by its all-leveling life, is essential to the preservation of human personality, and personality is essential to dignity, to decency, to hope. The clearest and simplest thing to be said about the Hebrew God, lofty and inaccessible Being, with whom nevertheless His purified and obedient children might have relationships, or about the "living God" of Greek theology, far removed from us but with whose deathless goodness, beauty and truth our mortality by some mediator may be endowed, is that the argument that supports such transcendence is the argument from necessity. It is the facts of experience, the very stuff of human life, coming down alike from Hebraic and Hellenic civilization, which demand Him. Immanence and transcendence are merely theistic terms for identity and difference. Through them is revealed and discovered personality, the "I" which is the ultimate fact of my consciousness. I can but reckon from the known to the unknown. The world which produced me is also, then, a cosmic identity and difference. In that double fact is found divine personality. But that aspect of His Person, that portion of the fact which feeds the imaginative and volitional life, is the glorious and saving unlikeness of God—His unthinkable and inexpressible glory; His utter comprehension and unbelievable compassion; His justice which knows no flaw and brooks no evasion and cannot be swerved; His power which may not be withstood and hence is a sure and certain tenderness; His hatred of sin, terrible and flaming, a hatred which will send sinful men through a thousand hells, if they will have them, and can only be saved thereby; His love for men, which is what makes Him hate their sin and leads Him by His very nature as God to walk into hell with the sinner, suffering with him a thousand times more than the sinner is able to understand or know,—like the Paul who could not wish himself, for himself, in hell, but who did wish himself accursed of God for his brethren's sake; like Jesus, who, in Gethsemane, would for Himself avoid His cross, but who accepted it and was willing to hang, forsaken of God, upon it, for the lives of men, identifying Himself to the uttermost with their fate. Yes; it is such a supernal God—that God who is apart, incredible, awful—that the soul of humanity craves and needs.

Of course, here again, as throughout these discussions, we are returning to a form of the old dualism. We cannot seem to help it. We may construct philosophies like Hegel's in which thesis and antithesis merge in a higher synthesis; we may use the dual view of the world as representing only a stage, a present achievement in cosmic progress or human understanding.

But that does not alter the incontestable witness of present experience that the religious consciousness is based upon, interwoven with, the sense of the cosmic division without, and the unresolved moral dualism within the individual life. It is important enough to remember, however, that we have rejected, at least for this generation, the old scholastic theologies founded on this general experience. Fashions of thought change with significant facility; there is not much of the Absolute about them! Nevertheless we cannot think with forgotten terms. Therefore ours is no mechanically divided world where man and God, nature and supernature, soul and body, belong to mutually exclusive territories. We do not deny the principle of identity. Hence we have discarded that old view of the world and all the elder doctrines of an absentee creator, a worthless and totally depraved humanity, a legalistic or substitutionary atonement, a magical and non-understandable Incarnation which flowed from it. But we are not discarding with them that other aspect of the truth, the principle of separateness, nor those value judgments, that perpetual vision of another nature, behind and beneath phenomena, from which the old dualism took its rise. It is the form which it assumed, the interpretation of experience which it gave, not the facts themselves, obscure but stubborn as they are, which it confessed, that we have dropped. Identity and difference are still here; man is a part of his world, but he is also apart from it. God is in nature and in us; God is without and other than nature and most awfully something other than us.

Indeed, the precise problem of the preacher today is to keep the old supernatural values and drop the old vocabulary with the philosophy which induced it. We must acknowledge the universe as one, and yet be able to show that the He or the It, beyond and without the world, is its only conceivable beginning, its only conceivable end, the chief hope of its brevity, the only stay of its idealism. It was the arbitrary and mechanical completeness of the old division, not the reality that underlay the distinction itself, which parted company with truth and hence lost the allegiance of the mind. It was that the old dualism tried to lock up this, the most baffling of all realities, in a formula,—that was what undid it. But we shall be equally foolish if now, in the interests of a new artificial clearness, we deny another portion of experience just as our fathers ignored certain other facts in the interests of their too well-defined systems. We cannot hold to the old world view which would bend the modern mind to the support of an inherited interpretation of experience and therefore would not any longer really explain or confirm it. Neither can we hold new views which mutilate the experience and leave out some of the most precious elements in it, even if in so doing we should simplify the problem for the mind. It would be an unreal simplification; it would darken, not illumine, the understanding; we should never rest in it. Nor do we need to be concerned if the intellect cannot perfectly order or easily demonstrate the whole of the religious life, fit each element with a self-verifying defense and explanation. No man of the world, to say nothing of a man of faith or imagination, has ever yet trusted to a purely intellectual judgment.

So we reject the old dualism, its dichotomized universe, its two sorts of authority, its prodigious and arbitrary supernaturalism. But we do not reject what lay behind it. Still we wrestle with the angel, lamed though we are by the contest, and we cannot let him go until the day breaks and the shadows flee away. It would be easier perhaps to give up the religious point of view, but for that ease we should pay with our life. For that swift answer, achieved by leaving out prime factors in the problem, we should be betraying the self for whose sake alone any answer is valuable. It does not pay to cut such Gordian knots! Our task, then, is to preach transcendence again, not in terms of the old absolutist philosophy, but in terms of the perceptions, the needs, the experience of the human heart and mind and will which produced that philosophy.

Nor is this so hard to do. Now, as always for the genuinely religious temperament, there are abundant riches of material lying ready to its hand. It is not difficult to make transcendence real and to reveal to men their consummate need of it when we speak of it in the language of experience and perception. What preaching should avoid is the abstractions of an archaic system of thought with all their provocative and contentious elements, the mingled dogmatism and incompleteness which any worked-out system contains. It is so foolish in the preacher to turn himself into a lay philosopher. Let him keep his insight clear, through moral discipline keep his intuitions high, his spirit pure, and then he can furnish the materials for philosophy.

Thus an almost universal trait of the religious temperament is in its delight in beauty. Sometimes it is repressed by an irreligious asceticism or narrowed and stunted by a literal and external faith. But when the religious man is left free, it is appropriate to his genius that he finds the world full of a high pleasure crowded with sound, color, fragrance, form, in which he takes exquisite delight. There is, in short, a serene and poetic naturalism, loosely called "nature-worship," which is keenly felt by both saints and sinners. All it needs for its consecration and perfection is to help men to see that this naturalism is vital and precious because, as a matter of fact, it is something more than naturalism, and more than pleasure objectified.

Recall, for instance, the splendors of the external world and that best season of our climate, the long, slow-breathing autumn. What high pleasure we take in those hushed days of mid-November in the soft brown turf of the uplands, the fragrant smell of mellow earth and burning leaves, the purple haze that dims and magnifies the quiescent hills. Who is not strangely moved by that profound and brooding peace into which Nature then gathers up the multitudinous strivings, the myriad activities of her life? Who does not love to lie, in those slow-waning days upon the sands which hold within their golden cup the murmuring and dreaming sea? The very amplitude of the natural world, its far-flung grace and loveliness, spread out in rolling moor and winding stream and stately forest marching up the mountain-side, subdues and elevates the spirit of a man.

Now, so it has always been and so men have always longed to be the worshipers of beauty. Therefore they have believed in a conscious and eternal Spirit behind it. Because again we know that personality is the only thing we have of absolute worth. A man cannot, therefore, worship beauty, wholly relinquish himself to its high delights, if he conceives of this majestic grace as impersonal and inanimate. For that which we worship must be greater than we. Behind it, therefore, just because it seems to us so beautiful, must be something that calls to the hidden deeps of the soul, something intimately akin to our own spirits. So man worships not nature, but the God of nature; senses an Eternal Presence behind all gracious form. For that interprets beauty and consecrates the spell of beauty over us. This gives a final meaning to what the soul perceives is an utter loveliness. This gives to beauty an eternal and cosmic significance commensurate to its charm and power. As long as men's hearts surge, too, when the tide yearns up the beach; as long as their souls become articulate when the birds sing in the dawn, and the flowers lift themselves to the sun; so long will men believe that only from a supreme and conscious Loveliness, a joyous and a gracious Spirit could have come the beauty which is so intimately related to the spirit of a man.

But not all saints and sinners are endowed with this joy and insight, this quick sensitiveness to beauty. Some of them cannot find the eternal and transcendent God in a loveliness which, by temperament, they either underrate or do not really see. There are a great many good people who cannot take beauty seriously. They become wooden and suspicious and uncomfortable whenever they are asked to perceive or enjoy a lovely object. Incredible though it seems, it appears to them to be unworthy of any final allegiance, any complete surrender, any unquestioning joy. But there are other ways in which they, too, may come to this sense of transcendence, other aspects of experience which also demand it. Most often it is just such folk who cannot perceive beauty, because they are practical or scientific or condemned to mean surroundings, who do feel to the full the grim force and terror of the external world. Prudence, caution, hard sense are to the fore with them! Very well; there, too, in these perceptions is an open door for the human spirit to transcend its environment, get out of its physical shell. The postulate of the absolute worth of beauty may be an argument for God drawn from subjective necessity. But the postulate of sovereign moral Being behind the tyranny and brutality of nature is an argument of objective necessity as well; here we all need God to explain the world.

For we deal with what certainly appear to be objective aspects of the truth, when we regard ourselves in our relation to the might of the physical universe. For even as men feed upon its beauty, so they have found it necessary to discover something which should enable them to live above and unafraid of its material and gigantic power. We have already seen how there appears to be a cosmic hostility to human life which sobers indeed those who are intelligent enough to perceive it. It is only the fool or the brute or the sentimentalist who is unterrified by nature. The man of reflection and imagination sees his race crawling ant-like over its tiny speck of slowly cooling earth and surrounded by titanic and ruthless forces which threaten at any moment to engulf it. The religious man knows that he is infinitely greater than the beasts of the field or the clods of the highway. Yet Vesuvius belches forth its liquid fire and in one day of stark terror the great city which was full of men is become mute and desolate. The proud liner scrapes along the surface of the frozen berg and crumples like a ship of cards. There is a splash, a cry, a white face, a lifted arm, and then all the pride and splendor, all the hopes and fears, the gorgeous dreams, the daring thoughts are gone. But the ice floats on unscarred and undeterred and the ocean tosses and heaves just as it did before.

Now, if this is all, if there is for us only the physical might of nature and the world is only what it seems to be; if there is no other God except such as can be found within this sort of cosmic process, then human life is a sardonic mockery, and self-respect a silly farce, and all the heroism of the heart and the valor of the mind the unmeaning activities of an insignificant atom. The very men who will naturally enter your churches are the ones who have always found that theory of life intolerable. It doesn't take in all the facts. They could not live by it and the soul of the race, looking out upon this universe of immeasurable material bulk, has challenged it and dared to assert its own superiority.

So by this road these men come back to the transcendent God without whom they cannot guard that integrity of personality which we are all set to keep. For here there is no way of believing in oneself, no way of enduring this world or our place in it and no tolerable way of understanding it except we look beneath this cosmic hostility and find our self-respect and a satisfying cosmic meaning in perceiving spiritual force, a conscious ethical purpose, which interpenetrates the thunder and the lightning, which lies behind the stars as they move in their perpetual courses. "Through it the most ancient heavens are fresh and strong." Integrity of personality in such a world as this, belief in self, without which life is dust and ashes in the mouth, rest on the sublime assumption that suffusing material force is ethical spirit, more like unto us than it, controlling force in the interest of moral and eternal purposes. In these purposes living, not mechanical, forces play a major part.

Of course, to all such reasoning the Kantians and humanists reply that these notions of an objective and eternal beauty, of a transcendent and actual Cosmic Being exist within the mind. They are purely subjective ideas, they are bounded by the inexorable circle of our experience, hence they offer no proof of any objective reality which may in greater or less degree correspond to them.

However, there must be a "source" of these ideas. To which the philosophers reply, Yes, they are "primitive and necessary," produced by reason only, without borrowing anything from the senses or the understanding. Yet there is no sufficient evidence that the idea of God is thus produced by any faculty of mind acting in entire freedom from external influence. On the contrary, the idea appears to owe much to the operation of external things upon the mind; it is not then the wholly unaffected product of reason. It is a response no less than an intuition. Like all knowledge a discovery, but the discovery of something there which could be discovered, hence, in that sense, a revelation.

It is not necessary, then, for men to meet their situation in the cosmos by saying with Kant: We will act as though there were a God, although we are always conscious that we have no real knowledge of Him as an external being. In the light of the tragic circumstances of humanity, this is demanding the impossible. No sane body of men will ever get sufficient inspiration for life or find an adequate solution for the problem of life by resting upon mere value judgments which they propose, by an effort of will, to put in the place of genuine reality judgments. Indeed, there is a truly scholastic naïveté, a sort of solemn and unconscious humor, in seriously proposing that men should vitalize and consecrate their deepest purposes and most difficult experiences by hypothesizing mere appearances and illusions.

Nor are we willing either to say with Santayana that all our sense of the beauty of the world is merely pleasure objectified and that we can infer no eternal Beauty from it. We are aware that there cannot be an immediate knowledge of a reality distinct from ourselves, that all our knowledge must be, in the nature of the case, an idea, a mental representation, that we can never know the Thing Itself. But if we believe, as we logically and reasonably may, that our subjective ideas are formed under the influence of objects unknown but without us, produced by stimuli, real, if not perceived apart from our own consciousness, then we may say that what we have is a mediate or representative knowledge not only of an Eternal Being but formed under the influence of that Being. Nor does the believer ask for more. He does not expect to see the King in His beauty; he only needs to know that He is, that He is there.

How self-verifying and moving, then, are the appeals ready to our hands. As long as man with the power to question, to strive, to aspire, to endure, to suffer, lives in a universe of ruthless and overwhelming might, so long, if he is to understand it or maintain his reason and his dignity, he will believe it to be controlled by a Spirit beyond no less than within, from whom his spirit is derived. It is out of the struggle to revere and conserve human personality, out of the belief in the indefectible worth and honor of selfhood that our race has fronted a universe in arms, and pitting its soul against nature has cried, "God is my refuge: underneath me, at the very moment when I am engulfed in earthquake shock or shattered in the battle's roar, there are everlasting arms!" There is something which is too deep for tears in the unconquerable idealism, the utter magnanimity of the faith of the human spirit in that which will answer to itself, as evidenced in this forlorn and glorious adventure of the soul. Sometimes we are constrained to ask ourselves, How can the heart of man go so undismayed through the waste places of the world?

But, of course, the preacher's main task is to interpret man's moral experience, which drives him out to search for the eternal in the terms of the "other" and redeeming God. We have spoken of the depersonalizing of religion which paganism and humanism alike have brought upon the world. One evidence of that has been the way in which we have confounded the social expressions of religion with its individual source. We are so concerned with the effect of our religion upon the community that we have forgotten that the heart of religion is found in the solitary soul. All of which means that we have here again yielded to the time spirit that enfolds us and have come to think of man as religious if he be humane. But that is not true. No man is ever religious until he becomes devout. And indeed no man of our sort—the saint and sinner sort—is ever long and truly humane unless the springs of his tenderness for men are found in his ever widening and deepening gratitude to God! Hence no man was ever yet able to preach the living God until he understood that the central need in human life is to reconcile the individual conscience to itself, compose the anarchy of the spiritual life. Men want to be happy and be fed; but men must have inward peace.

We swing back, therefore, to the native ground of preaching, approach the religious problem, now, not from the aesthetic or the scientific, but from the moral angle. Here we are dealing with the most poignant of all human experiences. For it is in this intensely personal world of moral failure and divided will that men are most acutely aware of themselves and hence of their need of that other-than-self beyond. The sentimental idealizing of contemporary life, the declension of the humanist's optimism into that superficial complacency which will not see what it does not like or what it is not expedient to see, makes one's mind to chuckle while one's heart doth ache. There is a brief heyday, its continuance dependent upon the uncontrollable factors of outward prosperity, physical and nervous vigor, capacity for preoccupation with the successive novelties of a diversified and complicated civilization, in which even men of religious temperament can minimize or ignore, perhaps sincerely disbelieve in, their divided life. Sometimes we think we may sin and be done with it. But always in the end man must come back to this moral tragedy of the soul. Because sin will not be done with us when we are done with it. Every evil is evil to him that does it and sooner or later we are compelled to understand that to be a sinner is the sorest and most certain punishment for sinning.

Then the awakening begins. Then can preaching stir the heart until deep answereth unto deep. It can talk of the struggle with moral temptation and weakness; of the unstable temperament which oscillates between the gutter and the stars; of the perversion or abuse of impulses good in themselves; of the dreadful dualism of the soul. For these are inheritances which have made life tragic in every generation for innumerable human beings. Whoever needed to explain to a company of grown men and women what the cry of the soul for its release from passion is? Every generation has its secret pessimists, brooding over the anarchy of the spirit, the issues of a distracted life. We need not ask with Faust, "Where is that place which men call 'Hell'?" nor wait for Mephistopheles to answer,

"Hell is in no set place, nor is it circumscribed,

For where we are—is Hell!"

Now, it is from such central and poignant experiences as these that men have been constrained to look outward for a God. For these mark the very disintegration of personality, the utter dissipation of selfhood. That is the inescapable horror of sin. That is what we mean when we say sinners are lost; so they are, they are lost to their own selves. With what discriminating truth the father in the parable of the lost boy speaks. "This, my son," he says, "was dead though he is alive again." So it is with us; being is the price we pay for sinning. The more we do wrong the less we are. How then shall we become alive again?

It is out of the shame and passion, the utter need of the human heart, which such considerations show to be real that men have built up their redemptive faiths. For all moral victory is conditioned upon help from without. To be sure each will and soul must strive desperately, even unto death, yet all that strife shall be in vain unless One stoops down from above and wrestles with us in the conflict. For the sinner must have two things, both of them beyond his unaided getting, or he will die. He must be released from his captivity. Who does not know the terrible restlessness, that grows and feeds upon itself and then does grow some more, of the man bound by evil and wanting to get out? The torture of sin is that it deprives us of the power to express ourselves. The cry of moral misery, therefore, is always the groaning of the prisoner. Oh, for help to break the bars of my intolerable and delicious sin that I may be myself once more! Oh, for some power greater than I which, being greater, can set me free!

But more than the sinner wants to be free does he want to be kept. Along with the passion for liberty is the desire for surrender. Again, then, he wants something outside himself, some Being so far above the world he lives in that it can take him, the whole of him, break his life, shake it to its foundations, then pacify, compose it, make it anew. He is so tired of his sin; he is so weary with striving; he wants to relinquish it all; get far away from what he is; flee like a bird to the mountain; lay down his life before the One like whom he would be. So he wants power, he wants peace. He would be himself, he would lose himself. He prays for freedom, he longs for captivity.

Now, out of these depths of human life, these vast antinomies of the spirit, has arisen man's belief in a Saviour-God. Sublime and awful are the sanctions upon which it rests. Out of the extremity and definiteness of our need we know that He must be and we know what He must be like. He is the One to whom all hearts are open, all desires known, from whom no secrets are hid. Who could state the mingling of desire and dread with which men strive after, and hide from, such a God? We want Him, yet until we have Him how we fear Him. For that inclusive knowledge of us which is God, if only we can bear to come to it, endows us with freedom. For then all the barriers are down, there is nothing to conceal, nothing to explain, nothing to hold back. Then reality and appearance coincide, character and condition correspond. I am what I am before Him. Supreme reality from without answers and completes my own, and makes me real, and my reality makes me free.

But if He thus knows me, and through that knowledge every inner inhibition melts in His presence and every damning secret's out, and all my life is spread like an open palm before His gaze, and I am come at last, through many weary roads, unto my very self, why then I can let go, I can relinquish myself. The dreadful tension's gone and in utter surrender the soul is poured out, until, spent and expressed, rest and peace flood back into the satisfied life. So the life is free; so the life is bound. So a man stands upon his feet; so he clings to the Rock that is higher than he. So the life is cleansed in burning light; so the soul is hid in the secret of God's presence. So men come to themselves; so men lose themselves in the Eternal. There is perfect freedom at last because we have attained to complete captivity. There is power accompanied by peace. That is the gift which the vision of a God, morally separate from, morally other than we, brings to the inward strife, the spiritual agony of the world. This is the need which that faith satisfies. It is, I suppose, in this exulting experience of moral freedom and spiritual peace which comes to those men who make the experiment of faith that they, for the most part, find their sufficient proof of the divine reality. Who ever doubted His existence who could cry with all that innumerable company of many kindreds and peoples and tongues:

"He brought me up also out of an horrible pit, out of the miry clay;

And he set my feet upon a rock, and established my goings.

And he hath put a new song in my mouth, even praise unto our God."

Here, then, is the preaching which is religious. How foolish are we not to preach it more! How trivial and impertinent it is to question the permanence of the religious interpretation of the world! What a revelation of personal insignificance it is to fail to revere the majesty of the devout and aspiring life! That which a starved and restless and giddy world has lost is this pool of quietness, this tower of strength, this cleansing grace of salvation, this haven of the Spirit. Belief in a transcendent deity is as natural as hunger and thirst, as necessary as sleep and breathing. It was the inner and essential needs of our fathers' lives which drove them out to search for Him. It will be the inner and essential needs of the lives of our children that shall bring them to the altar where their fathers and their fathers' fathers bowed down before them. Are we going to be afraid to keep its fires burning?

And so we come to our final and most difficult aspect of this transcendent problem. We have talked of the man who is separate from nature, and who knows himself as man because behind nature he sees the God from whom he is separate, too. We have seen how he needs that "otherness" in God to maintain his personality and how the gulf between him and that God induces that sense of helplessness which makes the humility and penitence of the religious life. We must come now to our final question. How is he to bridge the gulf? By what power can he go through with this experience we have just been relating and find his whole self in a whole world? How can he dare to try it? How can he gain power to achieve it?

Perhaps this is the central difficulty of all religion. It is certainly the one which the old Greeks felt. Plato, the father of Christian theology, and all neo-platonists, knew that the gulf is here between man and God and they knew that something or someone must bridge it for us. They perceived that man, unaided, cannot leap it at a stride. We proceed, driven by the facts of life, to the point where the soul looks up to the Eternal and confesses the kinship, and knows that only in His light shall it see light, and that it only shall be satisfied when it awakes in His likeness. But how shall the connection be made? What shall enable us to do that mystic thing, come back to God? We have frightful handicaps in the attempt. How shall the distrust that sin creates, the hardness that sin forms, the despair and helplessness that sin induces, the dreadful indifference which is its expression,—how shall they be removed? How shall the unfaith which the mystery, the suffering, the evil of the world induce be overcome? Being a sinner I do not dare, and being ignorant I do not believe, to come. God is there and God wants us; like as a father pitieth his children so He pitieth us. He knoweth our frame, He remembereth that we are dust. We know that is true; again we do not know it is true. All the sin that is in us and all which that sin has done to us insists and insists that it is not true. And the mind wonders—and wonders. What shall break that distrust; and melt away the hardness so that we have an open mind; and send hope into despair, hope with its accompanying confidence to act; change unfaith to belief, until, in having faith, we thereby have that which faith believes in? How amazing is life! We look out into the heavenly country, we long to walk therein, we have so little power to stir hand or foot to gain our entrance. We know it is there but all the facts of our rebellious or self-centered life, individual and associated alike, are against it and therefore we do not know that it is there.

Philosophy and reason and proofs of logic cannot greatly help us here. No man was ever yet argued into the kingdom of God. We cannot convince ourselves of our souls. For we are creatures, not minds; lives, not ideas. Only life can convince life; only a Person but, of course, a transcendent person that is more like Him than like us, can make that Other-who-lives certain and sure for us. This necessity for some intermediary who shall be a human yet more-than-human proof that God is and that man may be one with Him; this reinforcing of the old argument from subjective necessity by its verification in the actual stuff of objective life, has been everywhere sought by men.

Saviours, redeemers, mediators, then, are not theological manikins. They are not superfluous figures born of a mistaken notion of the universe. They are not secondary gods, concessions to our childishness. They, too, are called for in the nature of things. But to really mediate they must have the qualities of both that which they transmit and of those who receive the transmission. Most of all they must have that "other" quality, so triumphant and self-verifying that seeing it constrains belief. A mediator wholly unlike ourselves would be a meaningless and mocking figure. But a mediator who was chiefly like ourselves would be a contradiction in terms!

So we come back again to the old problem. Man needs some proof that he who knows that he is more than dust can meet with that other life from whose star his speck has been derived. Something has got to give him powerful reinforcement for this supreme effort of will, of faith. If only he could know that he and it ever have met in the fields of time and space, then he would be saved. For that would give him the will to believe; that would prove the ultimate; give him the blessed assurance which heals the wounds of the heart. Then he would have power to surrender. Then he would no longer fear the gulf, he would walk out onto it and know that as he walked he was with God.

Some such reasoning as this ought to make clear the place that Jesus holds in Christian preaching and why we call Him Saviour and why salvation comes for us who are of His spiritual lineage, through Him. Of course it is true that Jesus shows to all discerning eyes what man may be. But that is not the chief secret of His power; that is not why churches are built to Him and His cross still fronts, defeated but unconquerable, our pagan world. Jesus was more-than-nature and more-than-human. It is this "other" quality, operative and objectified in His experience within our world, which gives Him the absoluteness which makes Him indispensable and precious. The mystery is deepest here. For here we transfer the antinomy from thought to conduct; from inner perception to one Being's actual experience. Here, in Him, we say we see it resolved into its higher synthesis in actual operation.

Here, then, we can almost look into it. Yet when we do gaze, our eyes dazzle, our minds swerve, it is too much. It is not easy, indeed, at the present time it seems to be impossible to reconcile the Christ of history with the Christ of experience. Yet there would be neither right nor reason in saying that the former was more of a reality than the latter. And all the time the heart from which great thoughts arise, "the heart which has its reasons of which the mind knows nothing," says, Here in Him is the consummate quality, the absolute note of life. Here the impossible has been accomplished. Here the opposites meet and the contradictions blend. Here is something so incredible that it is true.

Of course, Jesus is of us and He is ours. That is true and it is inexpressibly sweet to remember it. Again, to use our old solecism, that is the lesser part of the truth; the greater part, for men of religion, is that Jesus is of God, that He belongs to Him. His chief office for our world has not been to show us what men can be like; it has been to give us the vision of the Eternal in a human face. For if He does reveal God to man then He must hold, as President Tucker says, the quality and substance of the life which He reveals.

Here is where He differs immeasurably from even a Socrates. What men want most to believe about Jesus is this, that when we commune with Him, we are with the infinite; that man's just perception of the Eternal Spirit, his desire to escape from time into reality, may be fulfilled in Jesus. That is the Gospel: Come unto Him, all ye that labor and are heavy laden, for He will give you rest. Whosoever drinketh of this water shall thirst again. But whosoever drinketh of the water that I shall give him shall never thirst; but the water that I shall give him shall be in him a well of water springing up into everlasting life. If the Son therefore shall make you free, you shall be free indeed.

Now, if all this is true, what is the religious preaching of Jesus, what aspect of His person meets the spiritual need? Clearly, it is His transcendence. It is not worthy of us to evade it because we cannot explain it. Surely what has hastened our present paganism has been the removal from the forefront of our consciousness of Jesus the Saviour, the divine Redeemer, the absolute Meeter of an absolute need. Of such preaching of Jesus we have today very little. The pendulum has swung far to the left, to the other exclusive emphasis, too obviously influenced by the currents of the day. It was perhaps inevitable that He should for a time drop out of His former place in Christian preaching under this combined humanistic and naturalistic movement. But it means that again we have relinquished those values which have made Jesus the heart of humanity.

Of course, He was a perfected human character inspired above all men by the spirit of God, showing the capacity of humanity to hold Divinity. This is what Mary celebrates in her paean, "He that is mighty has magnified me and holy is his name." But is this what men have passionately adored in Jesus? Has love of Him been self-love? Is this why He has become the sanctuary of humanity? I think not. We have for the moment no good language for the other conception of Him. He is indeed the pledge of what we may be, but how many of us would ever believe that pledge unless there was something else in Him, more than we, that guaranteed it? What, as President Tucker asks, is this power which shall make "maybe" into "is" for us? "Without doubt the trend of modern thought and faith is toward the more perfect identification of Christ with humanity. We cannot overestimate the advantage to Christianity of this tendency. The world must know and feel the humanity of Jesus. But it makes the greatest difference in result whether the ground of the common humanity is in Him or in us. To borrow the expressive language of Paul, was He 'created' in us? Or are we 'created' in Him? Grant the right of the affirmation that 'there is no difference in kind between the divine and the human'; allow the interchange of terms so that one may speak of the humanity of God and the divinity of man; appropriate the motive which lies in these attempts to bring God and man together and thus to explain the personality of Jesus Christ, it is still a matter of infinite concern whether His home is in the higher or the lower regions of divinity. After all, very little is gained by the transfer of terms. Humanity is in no way satisfied with its degree of divinity. We are still as anxious as ever to rise above ourselves and in this anxiety we want to know concerning our great helper, whether He has in Himself anything more than the possible increase of a common humanity. What is His power to lift and how long may it last? Shall we ever reach His level, become as divine as He, or does He have part in the absolute and infinite? This question may seem remote in result but it is everything in principle. The immanence of Christ has its present meaning and value because of His transcendence."[40]

Preaching today is not moving on the level of this discussion, is neither asking nor attempting to answer its questions. Great preaching in some way makes men see the end of the road, not merely the direction in which it travels. The power to do that we have lost if we have lost the more-than-us in Jesus. Humanity, unaided, cannot look to that end which shall explain the beginning. And does Jesus mean very much to us if He is only "Jesus"? Why do we answer the great invitation, "Come unto me"? Because He is something other than us? Because He calls us away from ourselves? back to home? Most of us no longer know how to preach on that plane of experience or from the point of view where such questions are serious and real. Our fathers had a world view and a philosophy which made such preaching easy. But their power did not lie in that world view; it lay in this vision of Jesus which produced the view. Is not this the vision which we need?

Footnote 40: (return)

"The Satisfaction of Humanity in Jesus Christ," *Andover Review*, January, 1893.

CHAPTER SEVEN
Worship as the Chief Approach to Transcendence

Whatever becomes the inward and the invisible grace of the Christian community such will be its outward and visible form. Those regulative ideas and characteristic emotions which determine in any age the quality of its religious experience will be certain to shape the nature and conduct of its ecclesiastical assemblies. Their influence will show, both in the liturgical and homiletical portions of public worship. If anything further were needed, therefore, to indicate the secularity of this age, its substitutes for worship and its characteristic type of preaching would, in themselves, reveal the situation. So we venture to devote these closing discussions to some observations on the present state of Protestant public worship and the prevailing type of Protestant preaching. For we may thus ascertain how far those ideas and perceptions which an age like ours needs are beginning to find an expression and what means may be taken to increase their influence through church services in the community.

We begin, then, in this chapter, not with preaching, but with worship. It seems to me clear that the chief office of the church is liturgical rather than homiletical. Or, if that is too technical a statement, it may be said that the church exists to set forth and foster the religious life and that, because of the nature of that life, it finds its chief opportunity for so doing in the imaginative rather than the rationalizing or practical areas of human expression. Even as Michael Angelo, at the risk of his life, purloined dead bodies that he might dissect them and learn anatomy, so all disciples of the art of religion need the discipline of intellectual analysis and of knowledge of the facts of the religious experience if they are to be leaders in faith. There is a toughness of fiber needed in religious people that can only come through such mental discipline. But anatomists are not sculptors. Michael Angelo was the genius, the creative artist, not because he understood anatomy, but chiefly because of those as yet indefinable and secret processes of feeling and intuition in man, which made him feel rather than understand the pity and the terror, the majesty and the pathos of the human spirit and reveal them in significant and expressive line. Knowledge supported rather than rivaled insight. In the same way, both saint and sinner need religious instruction. Nevertheless they are what they are because they are first perceptive rather than reasoning beings. They both owe, the one his salvation, the other his despair, to the fact that they have seen the vision of the holy universe. Both are seers; the saint has given his allegiance to the heavenly vision. The sinner has resolved to be disobedient unto it. Both find their first and more natural approach to religious truth, therefore, through the creative rather than the critical processes, the emotional rather than the informative powers.

There are, of course, many in our churches who would dissent from this opinion. It is characteristic of Protestantism, as of humanism in general, that it lays its chief emphasis upon the intelligence. If we go to church to practice the presence of God, must we not first know who and what this God is whose presence with us we are there asked to realize? So most Protestant services are more informative than inspirational. Their attendants are assembled to hear about God rather to taste and see that the Lord is good. They analyze the religious experience rather than enjoy it; insensibly they come to regard the spiritual life as a proposition to be proved, not a power to be appropriated. Hence our services generally consist of some "preliminary exercises," as we ourselves call them, leading up to the climax—when it is a climax—of the sermon.

Here is a major cause for the declension of the influence of Protestant church services. They go too much on the assumption that men already possess religion and that they come to church to discuss it rather than to have it provided. They call men to be listeners rather than participants in their temples. Of course, one may find God through the mind. The great scholar, the mathematician or the astronomer may cry with Kepler, "Behold, I think the thoughts of God after him!" Yet a service which places its chief emphasis upon the appeal to the will through instruction has declined from that realm of the absolutes where religion in its purest form belongs. For since preaching makes its appeal chiefly through reason, it thereby attempts to produce only a partial and relative experience in the life of the listener. It impinges upon the will by a slow process. Sometimes one gets so deadly weary of preaching because, in a world like ours, the reasonable process is so unreasonable. That's a half truth, of course, but one that the modern world needs to learn.

Others would dissent from our position by saying that service, the life of good will, is a sufficient worship. The highest adoration is to visit the widows and the fatherless in their affliction. *Laborare est orare.* What we do speaks so loud God does not care for what we say. True: but the value of what we do for God depends upon the godliness of the doer and where shall he find that godliness save in the secret place of the Most High? And the greatest gift we can give our fellows is to bring them into the divine presence. "There is," says Dr. William Adams Brown, "a service that is directed to the satisfaction of needs already in existence, and there is a service that is itself the creator of new needs which enlarge the capacity of the man to whom it would minister. To this larger service religion is committed, and the measure of a man's fitness to render it is his capacity for worship." But no one can give more than he has. If we are to offer such gifts we must ourselves go before and lead. To create the atmosphere in which the things of righteousness and holiness seem to be naturally exalted above the physical, the commercial, the domestic affairs of men; to lift the level of thought and feeling to that high place where the spiritual consciousness contributes its insights and finds a magnanimous utterance—is there anything that our world needs more? There are noble and necessary ministries to the body and the mind, but most needed, and least often offered, there is a ministry to the human spirit. This is the gift which the worshiper can bring. Knowledge of God may not be merely or even chiefly comprehended in a concept of the intelligence; knowledge of Him is that vitalizing consciousness of the Presence felt in the heart, which opens our eyes that we may see that the mountain is full of horses and chariots of fire round about us and that they who fight with us are more than they who fight with them. This is the true and central knowledge that private devotion and public worship alone can give; preaching can but conserve and transmit this religious experience through the mind, worship creates it in the heart. Edwards understood that neither thought nor conduct can take its place. "The sober performance of moral duty," said he, "is no substitute for passionate devotion to a Being with its occasional moments of joy and exaltation."

We should then begin with worship. A church which does not emphasize it before everything else is trying to build the structure of a spiritual society with the corner stone left out. Let us try, first of all, to define it. An old and popular definition of the descriptive sort says that "worship is the response of the soul to the consciousness of being in the presence of God." A more modern definition, analyzing the psychology of worship, defines it as "the unification of consciousness around the central controlling idea of God, the prevailing emotional tone being that of adoration." Evidently we mean, then, by worship the appeal to the religious will through feeling and the imagination. Worship is therefore essentially creative. Every act of worship seeks to bring forth then and there a direct experience of God through high and concentrated emotion. It fixes the attention upon Him as an object in Himself supremely desirable. The result of this unified consciousness is peace and the result of this peace and harmony is a new sense of power. Worship, then, is the attainment of that inward wholeness for which in one form or another all religion strives by means of contemplation. So by its very nature it belongs to the class of the absolutes.

Many psychologies of religion define this contemplation as aesthetic, and make worship a higher form of delight. This appears to me a quite typical non-religious interpretation of a religious experience. There are four words which need explaining when we talk of worship. They are: wonder, admiration, awe, reverence. Wonder springs from the recognition of the limitations of our knowledge; it is an experience of the mind. Admiration is the response of a growing intelligence to beauty, partly an aesthetic, partly an intellectual experience. These distinctions Coleridge had in mind in his well-known sentence "In wonder all philosophy began; in wonder it ends; and admiration fills up the interspace. But the first wonder is the offspring of ignorance; the last is the parent of adoration." Awe is the sense-perception of the stupendous power and magnitude of the universe; it is, quite literally, a godly fear. But it is not ignoble nor cringing, it is just and reasonable, the attitude, toward the Whole, of a comprehensive sanity.

Thus "I would love Thee, O God, if there were no heaven, *and if there were no hell, I would fear Thee no less.*" Reverence is devotion to goodness, sense of awe-struck loyalty to a Being manifestly under the influence of principles higher than our own.[41] Now it is with these last two, awe and reverence, rather than wonder and admiration, that worship has to do.

Hence the essence of worship is not aesthetic contemplation. Without doubt worship does gratify the aesthetic instinct and most properly so. There is no normal expression of man's nature which has not its accompanying delight. The higher and more inclusive the expression the more exquisite, of course, the delight. But that pleasure is the by-product, not the object, of worship. It itself springs partly from the awe of the infinite and eternal majesty which induces the desire to prostrate oneself before the Lord our Maker. "I have heard of Thee by the hearing of the ear: but now mine eye seeth Thee. Wherefore I abhor myself, and repent in dust and ashes." It also springs partly from passionate devotion of a loyal will to a holy Being. "Behold, as the eyes of servants look unto the hand of their masters and as the eyes of a maid unto the hand of her mistress; so our eyes wait upon the Lord." Thus reverence is the high and awe-struck hunger for spiritual communion. "My soul thirsteth for God, for the living God. When shall I come and appear before God?"

There is a noble illustration of the nature and the uses of worship in the Journals of Jonathan Edwards, distinguished alumnus of Yale College, and the greatest mind this hemisphere has produced. You remember what he wrote in them, as a youth, about the young woman who later became his wife: "They say there is a young lady in New Haven who is beloved of that great Being who made and rules the world, and that there are certain seasons in which this great Being in some way or other invisible comes to her and fills her mind with exceeding sweet delight, and that she hardly cares for anything except to meditate on Him. Therefore if you present all the world before her, with the richest of its treasures, she disregards and cares not for it and is unmindful of any pain or affliction. She has a strange sweetness in her mind, and singular purity in her affections, is most just and conscientious in all her conduct, and you could not persuade her to do anything wrong or sinful if you would give her all the world, lest she should offend this great Being. She is of wonderful calmness and universal benevolence of mind, especially after this great God has manifested Himself to her mind. She will sometimes go about from place to place singing sweetly and seems to be always full of joy and pleasure, and no one knows for what. She loves to be alone, walking in the fields and groves, and seems to have some one invisible always conversing with her."

Almost every element of worship is contained in this description. First, we have a young human being emotionally conscious of the presence of God, who in some way or other directly but invisibly comes to her. Secondly, we have her attention so fixed on the adoration of God that she hardly cares for anything except to meditate upon Him. Thirdly, as the result of this worshipful approach to religious reality, we have the profound peace and harmony, the *summum bonum* of existence, coupled with strong moral purpose which characterize her life. Here, then, is evidently the unification of consciousness in happy awe and the control of destiny through meditation upon infinite matters, that is, through reverent contemplation of God. Is it not one of those ironies of history wherewith fate is forever mocking and teasing the human spirit, that the grandson of this lady and of Jonathan Edwards should have been Aaron Burr?

Clearly, then, the end of worship is to present to the mind, through the imagination, one idea, majestic and inclusive. So it presents it chiefly through high and sustained feeling. Worship proceeds on the understanding that one idea, remaining almost unchanged and holding the attention for a considerable length of time, so directs the emotional processes that thought and action are harmonized with it. If one reads the great prayers of the centuries they indicate, for the most part, an unconscious understanding of this psychology of worship. Take, for instance, this noble prayer of Pusey's.

"Let me not seek out of Thee what I can find only in Thee, O Lord, peace and rest and joy and bliss, which abide only in thine abiding joy. Lift up my soul above the weary round of harassing thoughts, to Thy eternal presence. Lift up my soul to the pure, bright, serene, radiant atmosphere of Thy presence, that there I may breathe freely, there repose in Thy love, there be at rest from myself and from all things that weary me, and thence return arrayed with Thy peace, to do and bear what shall please Thee."

This prayer expresses the essence of worship which is the seeking, through the fixation of attention, not the delight but rather the peace and purity which can only be found in the consciousness of God. This peace is the necessary outcome of the indwelling presence. It ensues when man experiences the radiant atmosphere of the divine communion.

The same clear expression of worship is found in another familiar and noble prayer, that of Johann Arndt. Here, too, are phrases descriptive of a unified consciousness induced by reverent loyalty.

"Ah, Lord, to whom all hearts are open, Thou canst govern the vessel of my soul far better than can I. Arise, O Lord, and command the stormy wind and the troubled sea of my heart to be still, and at peace in Thee, that I may look up to Thee undisturbed and abide in union with Thee, my Lord. Let me not be carried hither and thither by wandering thoughts, but forgetting all else let me see and hear Thee. Renew my spirit, kindle in me Thy light that it may shine within me, and my heart burn in love and adoration for Thee. Let Thy Holy Spirit dwell in me continually, and make me Thy temple and sanctuary, and fill me with divine love and life and light, with devout and heavenly thoughts, with comfort and strength, with joy and peace."

Thus here one sees in the high contemplation of a transcendent God the subduing and elevating of the human will, the restoration and composure of the moral life. Finally, in a prayer of St. Anselm's there is a sort of analysis of the process of worship.

"O God, Thou *art* life, wisdom, truth, bounty and blessedness, the eternal, the only true Good. My God and my Lord, Thou art my hope and my heart's joy. I confess with thanksgiving that Thou hast made me in Thine image, that I may direct all my thoughts to Thee and love Thee. Lord, make me to know Thee aright that I may more and more love and enjoy and possess Thee."

One cannot conclude these examples of worshipful expression without quoting a prayer of Augustine, which is, I suppose, the most perfect brief petition in all the Christian literature of devotion and which gives the great psychologist's perception of the various steps in the unification of the soul with the eternal Spirit through sublime emotion.

"Grant, O God, that we may desire Thee, and desiring Thee, seek Thee, and seeking Thee, find Thee, and finding Thee, be satisfied with Thee forever."

I think one may see, then, why worship as distinct from preaching, or the hearing of preaching, is the first necessity of the religious life. It unites us as nothing else can do with God the whole and God the transcendent. The conception of God is the sum total of human needs and desires harmonized, unified, concretely expressed. It is the faith of the worshiper that this concept is derived from a real and objective Being in some way corresponding to it. No one can measure the influence of such an idea when it dominates the consciousness of any given period. It can create and set going new desires and habits, it can minish and repress old ones, because this idea carries, with its transcendent conception, the dynamic quality which belongs to the idea of perfect power. But this transcendent conception, being essentially of something beyond, without and above ourselves can only be "realized" through the feeling and the imagination, whose province it is to deal with the supersensuous values, with the fringes of understanding, with the farthest bounds of knowledge. These make the springboard, so to speak, from which man dares to launch himself into that sea of the infinite, which we can neither understand nor measure, but which nevertheless we may perceive and feel, which in some sense we know to be there.

So, if we deal first with worship, we are merely beginning at the beginning and starting at the bottom. And, in the light of this observation, it is appalling to survey the non-liturgical churches today and see the place that public devotion holds in them. It is not too much, I think, to speak of the collapse of worship in Protestant communities. No better evidence of this need be sought than in the nature of the present attempts to reinstate it. They have a naïveté, an incongruity, that can only be explained on the assumption of their impoverished background.

This situation shows first in the heterogeneous character of our experiments. We are continually printing on our churches' calendars what we usually call "programs," but which are meant to be orders of worship. We are also forever changing them. There is nothing inevitable about their order; they have no intelligible, self-verifying procedure. Anthems are inserted here and there without any sense of the progression or of the psychology of worship. Glorias are sung sometimes with the congregation standing up and sometimes while they are sitting down. There is no lectionary to determine a comprehensive and orderly reading of Scripture, not much sequence of thought or progress of devotion either in the read or the extempore prayers. There is no uniformity of posture. There are two historic attitudes of reverence when men are addressing the Almighty. They are the standing upon one's feet or the falling upon one's knees. For the most part we neither stand nor kneel; we usually loll. Some of us compromise by bending forward to the limiting of our breath and the discomfort of our digestion. It is too little inducive to physical ease or perhaps too derogatory to our dignity to kneel before the Lord our Maker. All this seems too much like the efforts of those who have forgotten what worship really is and are trying to find for it some comfortable or attractive substitute.

Second: we show our inexperience by betraying the confusion of aesthetic and ethical values as we strive for variety and entertainment in church services; we build them around wonder and admiration, not around reverence and awe. But we are mistaken if we suppose that men chiefly desire to be pleasantly entertained or extraordinarily delighted when they go into a church. They go there because they desire to enter a Holy Presence; they want to approach One before whom they can be still and know that He is God. All "enrichments" of a service injected into it here and there, designed to make it more attractive, to add color and variety, to arrest the attention of the senses are, as ends, beside the point, and our dependence upon them indicates the unhappy state of worship in our day. That we do thus make our professional music an end in itself is evident from our blatant way of advertising it. In the same way we advertise sermon themes, usually intended to startle the pious and provoke the ungodly. We want to arouse curiosity, social or political interest, to achieve some secular reaction. We don't advertise that tomorrow in our church there is to be a public worship of God, and that everything that we are going to do will be in the awe-struck sense that He is there. We are afraid that nobody would come if we merely did that!

What infidels we are! Why are we surprised that the world is passing us by? We say and we sing a great many things which it is incredible to suppose we would address to God if we really thought He were present. Yet anthems and congregational singing are either a sacrifice solemnly and joyously offered to God or else all the singing is less, and worse, than nothing in a church service. But how often sentimental and restless music, making not for restraint and reverence, not for the subduing of mind and heart but for the expression of those expansive and egotistical moods which are of the essence of romantic singing, is what we employ. There is a great deal of truly religious music, austere in tone, breathing restraint and reverence, quietly written. The anthems of Palestrina, Anerio, Viadana, Vittoria among the Italians; of Bach, Haydn, Handel, Mozart among the Germans; and of Tallis, Gibbons and Purcell among the English, are all of the truly devout order. Yet how seldom are the works of such men heard in our churches, even where they employ professional singers at substantial salaries. We are everywhere now trying to give our churches splendid and impressive physical accessories, making the architecture more and more stately and the pews more and more comfortable! Thus we attempt an amalgam of a mediaeval house of worship with an American domestic interior, adoring God at our ease, worshiping Him in armchairs, offering prostration of the spirit, so far as it can be achieved along with indolence of the body.

So we advertise and concertize and have silver vases and costly flowers and conventional ecclesiastical furniture. But we still hold a "small-and-early" in the vestibule before service and a "five o'clock" in the chapel afterward. Sunday morning church is a this-world function with a pietized gossip and a decorous sort of sociable with an intellectual fillip thrown in. Thus we try to make our services attractive to the secular instincts, the non-religious things, in man's nature. We try to get him into the church by saying, "You will find here what you find elsewhere." It's rather illogical. The church stands for something different. We say, "You will like to come and be one of us because we are not different." The answer is, "I can get the things of this world better in the world, where they belong, than with you." Thus we have naturalized our very offices of devotion! Hence the attempts to revive worship are incongruous and inconsistent. Hence they have that sentimental and accidental character which is the sign of the amateur. They do not bring us very near to the heavenly country. It might be well to remember that the servant of Jahweh doth not cry nor lift up his voice nor cause it to be heard in the streets.

Now, there are many reasons for this anomalous situation. One of them is our inheritance of a deep-rooted Puritan distrust of a liturgical service. That distrust is today a fetish and therefore much more potent that it was when it was a reason. Puritanism was born in the Reformation; it came out from the Roman church, where worship was regarded as an end in itself. To Catholic believers worship is a contribution to God, pleasing to Him apart from any effect it may have on the worshiper. Such a theory of it is, of course, open to grave abuse. Sometimes it led to indifference as to the effect of the worship upon the moral character of the communicant, so that worship could be used, not to conquer evil, but to make up for it, and thus sin became as safe as it was easy. Inevitably also such a theory of worship often degenerated into an utter formalism which made hypocrisy and unreality patent, until the *hoc est corpus* of the mass became the hocus-pocus of the scoffer.

Here is a reason, once valid because moral, for our present situation. Yet it must be confessed that again, as so often, we are doing what the Germans call "throwing out the baby with the bath," namely, repudiating a defect or the perversion of an excellence and, in so doing, throwing away that excellence itself. It is clear that no Protestant is ever tempted today to consider worship as its own reason and its own end. We are, in a sense, utilitarian ritualists. Worship to us is as valuable as it is valid because it is the chief avenue of spiritual insight, a chief means of awakening penitence, obtaining forgiveness, growing in grace and love. These are the ultimates; these are pleasing to God.

A second reason, however, for our situation is not ethical and essential, but economic and accidental. Our fathers' communities were a slender chain of frontier settlements, separated from an ancient civilization by an unknown and dangerous sea on the one hand, menaced by all the perils of a virgin wilderness upon the other. All their life was simple to the point of bareness; austere, reduced to the most elemental necessities. Inevitably the order of their worship corresponded to the order of their society. It is certain, I think, that the white meeting-house with its naked dignity, the old service with its heroic simplicity, conveyed to the primitive society which produced them elements both of high formality and conscious reverence which they could not possibly offer to our luxurious, sophisticated and wealthy age.

Is it not a dangerous thing to have brought an ever increasing formality and recognition of a developed and sophisticated community into our social and intellectual life but to have allowed our religious expression to remain so anachronistic? Largely for social and economic reasons we send most of our young men and young women to college. There we deliberately cultivate in them the perception of beauty, the sense of form, various expressions of the imaginative life. But how much has our average non-liturgical service to offer to their critically trained perceptions? Our church habits are pretty largely the transfer into the sanctuary of the hearty conventions of middle-class family life. The relations in life which are precious to such youth, the intimate, the mystical and subtle ones, get small recognition or expression. A hundred agencies outside the church are stimulating in the best boys and girls of the present generation fine sensibilities, critical standards, the higher hungers. Our services, chiefly instructive and didactic, informal and easy in character, irritate them and make them feel like truculent or uncomfortable misfits.

A third reason for the lack of corporate or public offices of devotion in our services lies in the intellectual character of the Protestant centuries. We have seen how they have been centuries of individualism. Character has been conceived of as largely a personal affair expressed in personal relationships. The believer was like Christian in Bunyan's *Pilgrim's Progress*. He started for the Heavenly Country because he was determined to save his own soul. When he realized that he was living in the City of Destruction it did not occur to him that, as a good man, he must identify his fate with it. On the contrary, he deserted wife and children with all possible expedition and got him out and went along through the Slough of Despond, up to the narrow gate, to start on the way of life. It was a chief glory of mediaeval society that it was based upon corporate relationships. Its cathedrals were possible because they were the common house of God for every element of the community. Family and class and state were dominant factors then. But we have seen how, in the Renaissance and the Romantic Movement, individualism supplanted these values. Now, Protestantism was contemporary with that new movement, indeed, a part of it. Its growing egotism and the colossal egotism of the modern world form a prime cause for the impoverishment of worship in Protestant churches.

And so this brings us, then, to the real reason for our devotional impotence, the one to which we referred in the opening sentences of the chapter. It is essentially due to the character of the regulative ideas of our age. It lies in that world view whose expressions in literature, philosophy and social organizations we have been reviewing in these pages. The partial notion of God which our age has unconsciously made the substitute for a comprehensive understanding of Him is essentially to blame. For since the contemporary doctrine is of His immanence, it therefore follows that it is chiefly through observation of the natural world and by interpretation of contemporary events that men will approach Him if they come to Him at all. Moreover, our humanism, in emphasizing the individual and exalting his self-sufficiency, has so far made the mood of worship alien and the need of it superfluous. The overemphasis upon preaching, the general passion of this generation for talk and then more talk, and then endless talk, is perfectly intelligible in view of the regulative ideas of this generation. It seeks its understanding of the world chiefly in terms of natural and tangible phenomena and chiefly by means either of critical observation or of analytic reasoning. Hence preaching, especially that sort which looks for the divine principle in contemporary events, has been to the fore. But worship, which finds the divine principle in something more and other than contemporary events—which indeed does not look outward to "events" at all—has been thrown into the background.

It seems to me clear, then, that if we are to emphasize the transcendent elements in religion; if they represent, as we have been contending, the central elements of the religious experience, its creative factors, then the revival of worship will be a prime step in creating a more truly spiritual society. I am convinced that a homilizing church belongs to a secularizing age. One cannot forget that the ultimate, I do not say the only, reason for the founding of the non-liturgical churches was the rise of humanism. One cannot fail to see the connection between humanistic doctrine and moralistic preaching, or between the naturalism of the moment and the mechanicalizing of the church. "The Christian congregation," said Luther, child of the humanistic movement, "should never assemble except the word of God be preached." "In other countries," says old Isaac Taylor, "the bell calls people to worship; in Scotland it calls them to a preachment." And one remembers the justice of Charles Kingsley's fling at the Dissenters that they were "creatures who went to church to hear sermons!" It would seem evident, then, that a renewal of worship would be the logical accompaniment of a return to distinctly religious values in society and church.

What can we do, then, better for an age of paganism than to cultivate this transcendent consciousness? Direct men away from God the universal and impersonal to God the particular and intimate. Nothing is more needed for our age than to insist upon the truth that there are both common and uncommon, both secular and sacred worlds; that these are not contradictory; that they are complementary; that they are not identical. It is the church's business to insist that men must live in the world of the sacred, the uncommon, the particular, in order to be able to surmount and endure the secular, the common and the universal. It is her business to insist that through worship all this can be accomplished. But can worship be taught? Is not the devotee, like the poet or the lover or any other genius, born and not made? Well, whether it can be taught or not, it at least can be cultivated and developed, and there are three very practical ways in which this cultivation can be brought about.

One of them is by paying intelligent attention to the physical surroundings of the worshiper. The assembly room for worship obviously should not be used for other purposes; all its suggestions and associations should be of one sort and that sort the highest. Quite aside from the question of taste, it is psychologically indefensible to use the same building, and especially the same room in the building, for concerts, for picture shows, for worship. Here we at once create a distracted consciousness; we dissipate attention; we deliberately make it harder for men and women to focus upon one, and that the most difficult, if the most precious, mood.

For the same reason, the physical form of the room should be one that does not suggest either the concert hall or the playhouse, but suggests rather a long and unbroken ecclesiastical tradition. Until the cinema was introduced into worship, we were vastly improving in these respects, but now we are turning the morning temple into an evening showhouse. I think we evince a most impertinent familiarity with the house of God! And too often the church is planned so that it has no privacies or recesses, but a hideous publicity pervades its every part. We adorn it with stenciled frescoes of the same patterns which we see in hotel lobbies and clubs; we hang up maps behind the reading desk; we clutter up its platform with grand pianos.

It is a mere matter of good taste and good psychology to begin our preparation for a ministry of worship by changing all this. There should be nothing in color or ornament which arouses the restless mood or distracts the eye. Severe and simple walls, restrained and devout figures in glass windows, are only to be tolerated. Descriptive windows, attempting in a most untractable medium a sort of naïve realism, are equally an aesthetic and an ecclesiastical offense. Figures of saints or great religious personages should be typical, impersonal, symbolic, not too much like this world and the things of it. There is a whole school of modern window glass distinguished by its opulence and its realism. It ought to be banished from houses of worship. Since it is the object of worship to fix the attention upon one thing and that thing the highest, the room where worship is held should have its own central object. It may be the Bible, idealized as the word of God; it may be the altar on which stands the Cross of the eternal sacrifice. But no church ought to be without one fixed point to which the eye of the body is insensibly drawn, thereby making it easier to follow it with the attention of the mind and the wishes of the heart. At the best, our Protestant ecclesiastical buildings are all empty! There are meeting-houses, not temples assembly rooms, not shrines. There is apparently no sense in which we are willing to acknowledge that the Presence is on their altar. But at least the attention of the worshiper within them may focus around some symbol of that Presence, may be fixed on some outward sign which will help the inward grace.

But second: our chief concern naturally must be with the content of the service of worship itself, not with its physical surroundings. And here then are two things which may be said. First, any formal order of worship should be historic; it should have its roots deep in the past; whatever else is true of a service of worship it ought not to suggest that it has been uncoupled from the rest of time and allowed to run wild. Now, this means that an order of worship, basing itself on the devotion of the ages, will use to some extent their forms. I do not see how anyone would wish to undertake to lead the same company of people week by week in divine worship without availing himself of the help of written prayers, great litanies, to strengthen and complement the spontaneous offices of devotion. There is something almost incredible to me in the assumption that one man can, supposedly unaided, lead a congregation in the emotional expression of its deepest life and desires without any assistance from the great sacramentaries and liturgies of the past. Christian literature is rich with a great body of collects, thanksgivings, confessions, various special petitions, which gather up the love and tears, the vision and the anguish of many generations. These, with their phrases made unspeakably precious with immemorial association, with their subtle fitting of phrase to insight, of expression to need, born of long centuries of experiment and aspiration, can do for a congregation what no man alone can ever hope to accomplish. The well of human needs and desires is so deep that, without these aids, we have not much to draw with, no plummet wherewith to sound its dark and hidden depths.

I doubt if we can overestimate the importance of giving this sense of continuity in petitions, of linking up the prayer of the moment and the worship of the day with the whole ageless process so that it seems a part of that volume of human life forever ascending unto the eternal spirit, just as the gray plume of smoke from the sacrifice ever curled upward morning by morning and night by night from the altar of the temple under the blue Syrian sky. We cannot easily give this sense of continuity, this prestige of antiquity, this resting back on a great body of experience, unless we know and use the language and the phrases of our fathers. It is to the God who hath been our dwelling place in all generations, that we pray; to Him who in days of old was a pillar of cloud by day and of fire by night to His faithful children; to the One who is the Ancient of Days, Infinite Watcher of the sons of men. Only by acquaintance with the phrases, the petitions of the past, and only by a liberal use of them can we give background and dignity, or anything approaching variety and completeness, to our own public expression and interpretation of the devotional life. If anyone objects to this use of formal prayers on the ground of their formality, let him remember that we, too, are formal, only we, alas, have made a cult of formlessness. It would surprise the average minister to know the well-worn road which his supposedly spontaneous and extempore devotions follow. Phrase after phrase following in the same order of ideas, and with the same pitiably limited vocabulary, appear week by week in them. How much better to enrich this painfully individualistic formalism with something of the corporate glories of the whole body of Christian believers.

But, second: there should be also the principle of immediacy in the service, room for the expression of individual needs and desires and for reference to the immediate and local circumstances of the believer. A church in which there is no spontaneous and extempore prayer, which only harked backward to the past, might build the tombs of the prophets but it might also stifle new voices for a new age. But extempore prayer should not be impromptu prayer. It should have coherence, dignity, progression. The spirit should have been humbly and painstakingly prepared for it so that sincere and ardent feeling may wing and vitalize its words. The great prayers of the ages, known of all the worshipers, perhaps repeated by them all together, tie in the individual soul to the great mass of humanity and it moves on, with its fellows, toward salvation as majestically and steadily as great rivers flow. The extempore and silent prayer, not unpremeditated but still the unformed outpouring of the individual heart, gives each man the consciousness of standing naked and alone before his God. Both these, the corporate and the separate elements of worships are vital; there should be a place for each in every true order of worship.

But, of course, the final thing to say is the first thing. Whatever may be the means that worship employs, its purpose must be to make and keep the church a place of repose, to induce constantly the life of relinquishment to God, of reverence and meditation. And this it will do as it seeks to draw men up to the "otherness," the majesty, the aloofness, the transcendence of the Almighty. To this end I would use whatever outward aids time and experience have shown will strengthen and deepen the spiritual understanding. I should not fear to use the cross, the sacraments, the kneeling posture, the great picture, the carving, the recitation of prayers and hymns, not alone to intensify this sense in the believer but equally to create it in the non-believer. The external world moulds the internal, even as the internal makes the external. If these things mean little in the beginning, there is still truth in the assertion of the devotee that if you practice them they will begin to mean something to you. This is not merely that a meaning will be self-induced. It is more than that. They will put us in the volitional attitude, the emotional mood, where the meaning is able to penetrate. Just as all the world acknowledges that there is an essential connection between good manners and good morals, between military discipline and physical courage, so there is a connection between a devotional service and the gifts of the spiritual life. Such a service not merely strengthens belief in the High and Holy One, it has a real office in creating, in making possible, that belief itself.

We shall sum it all up if we say in one word that the offices of devotion emphasize the cosmic character of religion. They take us out of the world of moral theism into the world of a universal theism. They draw us away from religion in action to religion in itself; they give us, not the God of this world, but the God who is from everlasting to everlasting, to whom a thousand years are but as yesterday when it is past and as a watch in the night. Thus they help us to make for ourselves an interior refuge into whose precincts no eye may look, into whose life no other soul may venture. In that refuge we can be still and know that He is God. There we can eat the meat which the world knoweth not of, there have peace with Him. It is in these central solitudes, induced by worship, that the vision is clarified, the perspective corrected, the vital forces recharged. Those who possess them are transmitters of such heavenly messages; they issue from them as rivers pour from undiminished mountain streams. Does the world's sin and pain and weakness come and empty itself into the broad current of these devout lives? Then their fearless onsweeping forces gather it all up, carry it on, cleanse and purify it in the process. Over such lives the things of this world have no power. They are kept secretly from them all in His pavilion where there is no strife of tongues.

Footnote 41: (return)

For a discussion of these four words see Allen, *Reverence as the Heart of Christianity*, pp. 253 ff.

CHAPTER EIGHT
Worship and the Discipline of Doctrine

If one were to ask any sermon-taster of our generation what is the prevailing type of discourse among the better-known preachers of the day, he would probably answer, "The expository." Expository preaching has had a notable revival in the last three decades, especially among liberal preachers; that is, among those who like ourselves have discarded scholastic theologies, turned to the ethical aspects of religion for our chief interests and accepted the modern view of the Bible. To be sure, it is not the same sort of expository preaching which made the Scottish pulpit of the nineteenth century famous. It is not the detailed exposition of each word and clause, almost of each comma, which marks the mingled insight and literalism of a Chalmers, an Alexander Maclaren, a Taylor of the Broadway Tabernacle. For that assumed a verbally inspired and hence an inerrant Scripture; it dealt with the literature of the Old and New Testaments as being divine revelations. The new expository preaching proceeds from almost an opposite point of view. It deals with this literature as being a transcript of human experience. Its method is direct and simple and, within sharp limits, very effective. The introduction to one of these modern expository sermons would run about as follows:

"I suppose that what has given to the Old and New Testament Scriptures their enduring hold over the minds and consciences of men has been their extraordinary humanity. They contain so many vivid and accurate recitals of typical human experience, portrayed with self-verifying insight and interpreted with consummate understanding of the issues of the heart. And since it is true, as Goethe said, 'That while mankind is always progressing man himself remains ever the same,' and we are not essentially different from the folk who lived a hundred generations ago under the sunny Palestinian sky, we read these ancient tales and find in them a mirror which reflects the lineaments of our own time. For instance,..."

Then the sermonizer proceeds to relate some famous Bible story, resolving its naïve Semitic theophanies, its pictorial narration, its primitive morality, into the terms of contemporary ethical or political or economic principles. Take, for instance, the account of the miracle of Moses and the Burning Bush. The preacher will point out that Moses saw a bush that burned and burned and that, unlike most furze bushes of those upland pastures which were ignited by the hot Syrian sun, was not consumed. It was this enduring quality of the bush that interested him. Thus Moses showed the first characteristic of genius, namely, capacity for accurate and discriminating observation. And he coupled this with the scientific habit of mind. For he said, "I will now turn aside and see why!" Thus did he propose to pierce behind the event to the cause of the event, behind the movement to the principle of the movement. What a modern man this Moses was! It seems almost too good to be true!

But as yet we have merely scratched the surface of the story. For he took his shoes from off his feet when he inspected this new phenomenon, feeling instinctively that he was on holy ground. Thus there mingled with his scientific curiosity the second great quality of genius, which is reverence. There was no complacency here but an approach to life at once eager and humble; keen yet teachable and mild. And now behold what happens! As a result of this combination of qualities there came to Moses the vision of what he might do to lead his oppressed countrymen out of their industrial bondage. Whereupon he displayed the typical human reaction and cried, "Who am I, that I should go unto Pharoah or that I should lead the children of Israel out of Egypt!" My brother Aaron, who is an eloquent person—and as it turned out later also a specious one—is far better suited for this undertaking. Thus he endeavored to evade the task and cried, "Let someone else do it!" Having thus expounded the word of God (!) the sermon proceeds to its final division in the application of this shrewd and practical wisdom to some current event or parochial situation.

Now, such preaching is indubitably effective and not wholly illegitimate. Its technique is easily acquired. It makes us realize that the early Church Fathers, who displayed a truly appalling ingenuity in allegorizing the Old Testament and who found "types" of Christ and His Church in frankly sensual Oriental wedding songs, have many sturdy descendants among us to this very hour! Such preaching gives picturesqueness and color, it provides the necessary sugar coating to the large pill of practical and ethical exhortation. To be sure, it does not sound like the preaching of our fathers. The old sermon titles—"Suffering with Christ that we may be also glorified with Him," for instance—seem very far away from it. Nor is it to be supposed that this is what its author intended the story we have been using to convey nor that these were the reactions that it aroused in the breasts of its original hearers. But as the sermonizer would doubtless go on to remark, there is a certain universal quality in all great literature, and genius builds better than it knows, and so each man can draw his own water of refreshment from these great wells of the past. And indeed nothing is more amazing or disconcerting than the mutually exclusive notions, the apparently opposing truths, which can be educed by this method, from one and the same passage of Scripture! There is scarcely a chapter in all the Old Testament, and to a less degree in the New Testament, which may not be thus ingeniously transmogrified to meet almost any homiletical emergency.

Now, I may as well confess that I have preached this kind of sermon lo! these many years *ad infinitum* and I doubt not *ad nauseam*. We have all used in this way the flaming rhetoric of the Hebrew prophets until we think of them chiefly as indicters of a social order. They were not chiefly this but something quite different and more valuable, namely, religious geniuses. First-rate preaching would deal with Amos as the pioneer in ethical monotheism, with Hosea as the first poet of the divine grace, with Jeremiah as the herald of the possibility of each man's separate and personal communion with the living God. But, of course, such religious preaching, dealing with great doctrines of faith, would have a kind of large remoteness about it; it would pay very little attention to the incidents of the story, and indeed, would tend to be hardly expository at all, but rather speculative and doctrinal.

And that brings us to the theme of this final discussion. For I am one of those who believe that great preaching is doctrinal preaching and that it is particularly needed at this hour. The comparative neglect of the New Testament in favor of the Old in contemporary preaching; the use and nature of the expository method—no less than the unworshipful character of our services—appear to me to offer a final and conclusive proof of the unreligious overhumanistic emphases of our interpretation of religion. And if we are to have a religious revival, then it seems to me worshipful services must be accompanied by speculative preaching and I doubt if the one can be nobly maintained without the other. For we saw that worship is the direct experience of the Absolute through high and concentrated feeling. Even so speculative and, in general, doctrinal preaching is the same return to first principles and to ultimate values in the realm of ideas. It turns away from the immediate, the practical, the relative to the final and absolute in the domain of thought.

Now, obviously, then, devout services and doctrinal preaching should go together. No high and persistent emotions can be maintained without clear thinking to nourish and steady them. There is in doctrinal preaching a certain indifference to immediate issues; to detailed applications. It deals, by its nature, with comprehensive and abstract rather than local and concrete thinking; with inclusive feeling, transcendent aspiration. It does not try to pietize the ordinary, commercial and domestic affairs of men. Instead it deals with the highest questions and perceptions of human life; argues from those sublime hypotheses which are the very subsoil of the religious temperament and understanding. It deals with those aspects of human life which indeed include, but include because they transcend, the commercial and domestic, the professional and political affairs of daily living. We have been insisting in these chapters that it is that portion of human need and experience which lies between the knowable and the unknowable with which it is the preacher's chief province to deal. Doctrinal preaching endeavors to give form and relations to its intuitions and high desires, its unattainable longings and insights. There is a native alliance between the doctrine of Immanence and expository preaching. For the office of both is to give us the God of this world in the affairs of the moment. There is a native alliance between expository preaching and humanism which very largely accounts for the latter's popularity. For expository preaching, as at present practiced, deals mostly with ethical and practical issues, with the setting of the house of this world in order. There is also a native and majestic alliance between the idea of transcendence and doctrinal preaching and between the facts of the religious experience and the content of speculative philosophy. Not pragmatism but pure metaphysics is the native language of the mind when it moves in the spiritual world.

But I am aware that already I have lost my reader's sympathy. You do not desire to preach doctrinal sermons and while you may read with amiable patience and faintly smiling complacency this discussion, you have no intention of following its advice. We tend to think that doctrinal sermons are outmoded—old-fashioned and unpopular—and we dread as we dread few other things, not being up to date. Besides, doctrinal preaching offers little of that opportunity which is found in expository and yet more in topical preaching for exploiting our own personalities. Some of us are young. It is merely a polite way of saying that we are egotistical. We know in our secret heart of hearts that the main thing that we have to give the world is our own new, fresh selves with their corrected and arresting understanding of the world. We are modestly yet eagerly ready to bestow that gift of ours upon the waiting congregation. One of the few compensations of growing old is that, as the hot inner fires burn lower, this self-absorption lessens and we become disinterested and judicial observers of life and find so much pleasure in other people's successes and so much wisdom in other folk's ideas. But not so for youth; it isn't what the past or the collective mind and heart have formulated: it's what you've got to say that interests you. Hence it is probably true that doctrinal preaching, in the very nature of things, makes no strong appeal to men who are beginning the ministry.

But there are other objections which are more serious, because inherent in the very genius of doctrinal preaching itself. First: such preaching is more or less remote from contemporary and practical issues. It deals with thought, not actions; understanding rather than efficiency; principles rather than applications. It moves among the basic concepts of the religious life; deals with matters beyond and above and without the tumultuous issues of the moment. So it follows that doctrinal preaching has an air of detachment, almost of seclusion from the world; the preacher brings his message from some pale world of ideas to this quick world of action. And we are afraid of this detachment, the abstract and theoretical nature of the thinker's sermon.

I think the fear is not well grounded. What is the use of preaching social service to the almost total neglect of setting forth the intellectual and emotional concept of the servant? It is the quality of the doer which determines the value of the deed. Why keep on insisting upon being good if our hearers have never been carefully instructed in the nature and the sanctions of goodness? Has not the trouble with most of our political and moral reform been that we have had a passion for it but very little science of it? How can we know the ways of godliness if we take God Himself for granted? No: our chief business, as preachers, is to preach the content rather than the application of the truth. Not many people are interested in trying to find the substance of the truth. It is hated as impractical by the multitude of the impatient, and despised as old-fashioned by the get-saved-quick reformers. Nevertheless we must find out the distinctions between divine and human, right and wrong, and why they are what they are, and what is the good of it all. There is no more valuable service which the preacher can render his community than to deliberately seclude himself from continual contact with immediate issues and dwell on the eternal verities. When Darwin published *The Descent of Man* at the end of the Franco-Prussian War, the *London Times* took him severely to task for his absorption in purely scientific interests and hypothetical issues. "When the foundations of property and the established order were threatened with the fires of the Paris Commune; when the Tuileries were burning—how could a British subject be occupying himself with speculations in natural science in no wise calculated to bring aid or comfort to those who had a stake in the country!" Well, few of us imagine today that Darwin would have been wise to have exchanged the seclusion and the impractical hours of the study for the office or the camp, the market or the street.

Yet the same fear of occupying ourselves with central and abstract matters still obsesses us. At the Quadrennial Conference of the Methodist Episcopal Church held recently at Des Moines, thirty-four bishops submitted an address in which they said among other things: "Of course, the church must stand in unflinching, uncompromising denunciation of all violations of laws, against all murderous child labor, all foul sweat shops, all unsafe mines, all deadly tenements, all excessive hours for those who toil, all profligate luxuries, all standards of wage and life below the living standard, all unfairness and harshness of conditions, all brutal exactions, whether of the employer or union, all overlordships, whether of capital or labor, all godless profiteering, whether in food, clothing, profits or wages, against all inhumanity, injustice and blighting inequality, against all class-minded men who demand special privileges or exceptions on behalf of their class."

These are all vital matters, yet I cannot believe that it is the church's chief business thus to turn her energies to the problems of the material world. This would be a stupendous program, even if complete in itself; as an item in a program it becomes almost a *reductio ad absurdum*. The *Springfield Republican* in an editorial comment upon it said: "It fairly invites the question whether the church is not in some danger of trying to do too much. The fund of energy available for any human undertaking is not unlimited; energy turned in one direction must of necessity be withdrawn from another and energy diffused in many directions cannot be concentrated. Count the adjectives—'murderous,' 'foul,' 'unsafe,' 'deadly,' 'excessive,' 'profligate,' 'brutal,' 'godless,' 'blighting'—does not each involve research, investigation, comparison, analysis, deliberation, a heavy tax upon the intellectual resources of the church if any result worth having is to be obtained? Can this energy be found without subtracting energy from some other sphere?"

The gravest problems of the world are not found here. They are found in the decline of spiritual understanding, the decay of moral standards, the growth of the vindictive and unforgiving spirit, the lapse from charity, the overweening pride of the human heart. With these matters the church must chiefly deal; to their spiritual infidelity she must bring a spiritual message; to their poor thinking she must bring the wisdom of the eternal. This task, preventive not remedial, is her characteristic one. Is it not worth while to remember that the great religious leaders have generally ignored contemporary social problems? So have the great artists who are closely allied to them. Neither William Shakespeare nor Leonardo da Vinci were reformers; neither Gautama nor the Lord Jesus had much to say about the actual international economic and political readjustments which were as pressing in their day as ours. They were content to preach the truth, sure that it, once understood, would set men free.

But a second reason why we dislike doctrinal preaching is because we confound it with dogmatic preaching. Doctrinal sermons are those which deal with the philosophy of religion. They expound or defend or relate the intellectual statements, the formulae of religion. Such discourses differ essentially from dogmatic sermonizing. For what is a doctrine? A doctrine is an intellectual formulation of an experience. Suppose a man receives a new influx of moral energy and spiritual insight, through reading the Bible, through trying to pray, through loving and meditating upon the Lord Jesus. That experience isn't a speculative proposition, it isn't a faith or an hypothesis; it's a fact. Like the man in the Johannine record the believer says, "Whether he be a sinner I know not: but one thing I know, that, whereas I was blind, now I see."

Now, let this new experience of moral power and spiritual insight express itself, as it normally will, in a more holy and more useful life, in the appropriate terms of action. There you get that confession of experience which we call character. Or let it express itself in the appropriate emotions of joy and awe and reverence so that, like Ray Palmer, the convert writes an immortal hymn, or a body of converts like the early church produces the *Te Deum*. There is the confession of experience in worship. Or let a man filled with this new life desire to understand it; see what its implications are regarding the nature of God, the nature of man, the place of Christ in the scale of created or uncreated Being. Let him desire to thus conserve and interpret that he may transmit this new experience. Then he will begin to define it and to reduce it, for brevity and clearness, to some abstract and compact formula. Thus he will make a confession of experience in doctrine.

Doctrines, then, are not arbitrary but natural, not accidental but essential. They are the hypotheses regarding the eternal nature of things drawn from the data of our moral and spiritual experience. They are to religion just what the science of electricity is to a trolley car, or what the formula of evolution is to natural science, or what the doctrine of the conservation of energy is, or was, to physics. Doctrines are signposts; they are placards, index fingers, notices summing up and commending the proved essences of religious experience. Two things are always true of sound doctrine. First: it is not considered to have primary value; its worth is in the experience to which it witnesses. Second: it is not fixed but flexible and progressive. Someone has railed at theology, defining it as the history of discarded errors. That is a truth and a great compliment and the definition holds good of the record of any other science.

Now, if doctrines are signposts, dogmas are old and now misleading milestones. For what is a dogma? It may be one of two things. Usually it is a doctrine that has forgotten that it ever had a history; a formula which once had authority because it was a genuine interpretation of experience but which now is so outmoded in fashion of thought, or so maladjusted to our present scale of values, as to be no longer clearly related to experience and is therefore accepted merely on command, or on the prestige of its antiquity. Or it may be a doctrine promulgated *ex cathedra*, not because religious experience produced it, but because ecclesiastical expediencies demand it. Thus, to illustrate the first sort of dogma, there was once a doctrine of the Virgin Birth. Men found, as they still do, both God and man in Jesus; they discovered when they followed Him their own real humanity and true divinity. They tried to explain and formalize the experience and made a doctrine which, for the circle of ideas and the extent of the factual knowledge of the times, was both reasonable and valuable. The experience still remains, but the doctrine is no longer psychologically or biologically credible. It no longer offers a tenable explanation; it is not a valuable or illuminating interpretation. Hence if we hold it at all today, it is either for sentiment or for the sake of mere tradition, namely, for reasons other than its intellectual usefulness or its inherent intelligibility. So held it passes over from doctrine into dogma. Or take, as an example of the second sort, the dogma of the Immaculate Conception, promulgated by Pius IX in the year 1854, and designed to strengthen the prestige of the Papal See among the Catholic powers of Europe and to prolong its hold upon its temporal possessions. De Cesare describes the promulgation of the dogma as follows:

"The festival on that day, December 8, 1854, sacred to the Virgin, was magnificent. After chanting the Gospel, first in Latin, then in Greek, Cardinal Macchi, deacon of the Sacred College, together with the senior archbishops and bishops present, all approached the Papal throne, pronouncing these words in Latin, 'Deign, most Holy Father, to lift your Apostolic voice and pronounce the dogmatic Decree of the Immaculate Conception, on account of which there will be praise in heaven and rejoicings on earth.' The Pope replying, stated that he welcomed the wish of the Sacred College, the episcopate, the clergy, and declared it was essential first of all to invoke the help of the Holy Spirit. So saying he intoned *in Veni Creator*, chanted in chorus by all present. The chant concluded, amid a solemn silence Pius IX's finely modulated voice read the following Decree:

"'It shall be Dogma, that the most Blessed Virgin Mary, in the first instant of the Conception, by singular privilege and grace of God, in virtue of the merits of Jesus Christ, the Saviour of mankind, was preserved from all stain of original sin.' The senior cardinal then prayed the Pope to make this Decree public, and, amid the roar of cannon from Fort St. Angelo and the festive ringing of church bells, the solemn act was accomplished.'"[42] Here is an assertion regarding Mary's Conception which has only the most tenuous connection with religious experience and which was pronounced for ecclesiastical and political reasons. Here we have dogma at its worst. Here, indeed, it is so bad as to resemble many of the current political and economic pronunciamentos!

Now, nobody wants dogmatic preaching, but there is nothing that we need more than we do doctrinal preaching and nothing which is more interesting. The specialization of knowledge has assigned to the preacher of religion a definite sphere. No amount of secondary expertness in politics or economics or social reform or even morals can atone for the abandonment of our own province. We are set to think about and expound religion and if we give that up we give up our place in a learned profession. Moreover, the new conditions of the modern world make doctrine imperative. That world is distinguished by its free inquiry, its cultivation of the scientific method, its abandonment of obscuranticisms and ambiguities. It demands, then, devout and holy thinking from us. Who would deny that the revival of intellectual authority and leadership in matters of religion is terribly needed in our day? Sabatier is right in saying that a religion without doctrine is a self-contradictory idea. Harnack is not wrong in saying that a Christianity without it is inconceivable.

And now I know you are thinking in your hearts, Well, what inconsistency this man shows! For a whole book he has been insisting on the prime values of imagination and feeling in religion and now he concludes with a plea for the thinker. But it is not so inconsistent as it appears. It is just because we do believe that the discovery, the expression and the rewards of religion lie chiefly in the superrational and poetic realms that therefore we want this intellectual content to accompany it, not supersede it, as a balancing influence, a steadying force. There are grave perils in worshipful services corresponding to their supreme values. Mystical preaching has the defects of its virtues and too often sinks into that vague sentimentalism which is the perversion of its excellence. How insensibly sometimes does high and precious feeling degenerate into a sort of religious hysteria! It needs then to be always tested and corrected by clear thinking.

But we in no way alter our original insistence that in our realm as preachers, unlike the scientist's realm of the theologians, thought is the handmaid, not the mistress. Our great plea, then, for doctrinal preaching is that by intellectual grappling with the final and speculative problems of religion we do not supersede but feed the emotional life and do not diminish but focus and steady it. It is that you and I may have reserves of feeling—indispensable to great preaching—sincerity and intensity of emotion, that disciplined imagination which is genius, that restrained passion which is art, and that our congregations may have the same, that we must strive for intellectual power, must do the preaching that gives people something to think about. These are the religious and devout reasons why we value intellectual honesty, precision of utterance, reserve of statement, logical and coherent thinking.

We are come, then, to the conclusion of our discussions. They have been intended to restore a neglected emphasis upon the imaginative and transcendent as distinguished from the ethical and humanistic aspects of the religious life. They have tried to show that the reaching out by worship to this "otherness" of God and to the ultimate in life is man's deepest hunger and the one we are chiefly set to feed. I am sure that the chief ally of the experience of the transcendence of God and the cultivation of the worshipful faculties in man is to be found in severe and speculative thinking. I believe our almost unmixed passion for piety, for action, for practical efficiency, betrays us. It indicates that we are trying to manufacture effects to conceal the absence of causes. We may look for a religious revival when men have so meditated upon and struggled with the fundamental ideas of religion that they feel profoundly its eternal mysteries.

And finally, we have the best historical grounds for our position. Sometimes great religious movements have been begun by unlearned and uncritical men like Peter the hermit or John Bunyan or Moody. But we must not infer from this that religious insight is naturally repressed by clear thinking or fostered by ignorance. Dr. Francis Greenwood Peabody has pointed out that the great religious epochs in Christian history are also epochs in the history of theology. The Pauline epistles, the *Confessions of Augustine*, the *Meditations* of Anselm, the *Simple Method of How to Pray* of Luther, the *Regula* of Loyola, the *Monologen* of Schleiermacher, these are all manuals of the devout life, they belong in the distinctively religious world of supersensuous and the transcendent, and one thing which accounts for them is that the men who produced them were religious geniuses because they were also theologians.[43]

It is to be remembered that we are not saying that the theologian makes the saint. I do not believe that. Devils can believe and tremble; Abelard was no saint. But we are contending that the great saint is extremely likely to be a theologian. Protestantism, Methodism, Tractarianism, were chiefly religious movements, interested in the kind of questions and moved by the sorts of motives which we have been talking about. They all began within the precincts of universities. Moreover, the Lord Jesus, consummate mystic, incomparable artist, was such partly because He was a great theologian as well. His dealings with scribe and Pharisee furnish some of the world's best examples of acute and courageous dialectics. His theological method differed markedly from the academicians of His day. Nevertheless it was noted that He spoke with an extraordinary authority. "He gave," as Dr. Peabody also points out, "new scope and significance to the thought of God, to the nature of man, to the destiny of the soul, to the meaning of the world. He would have been reckoned among the world's great theologians if other endowments had not given Him a higher title."[44]

It is a higher title to have been the supreme mystic, the perfect seer. All I have been trying to say is that it is to these sorts of excellencies that the preacher aspires. But the life of Jesus supremely sanctions the conviction that preaching upon high and abstract and even speculative themes and a rigorous intellectual discipline are chief accompaniments, appropriate and indispensable aids, to religious insight and to the cultivating of worshipful feeling. So we close our discussions with the supreme name upon our lips, leaving the most fragrant memory, the clearest picture, remembering Him who struck the highest note. It is to His life and teaching that we humbly turn to find the final sanction for the distinctively religious values. Who else, indeed, has the words of Eternal Life?

Footnote 42: (return)

The Last Days of Papal Rome, pp. 127 ff.

Footnote 43: (return)

See the "Call to Theology," *Har. Theo. Rev.*, vol. I, no. 1, pp. 1 ff.

Footnote 44: (return)

"Call to Theology," *Har. Theo. Rev.*, vol. I, no. 1, p. 8.

Milton Keynes UK
Ingram Content Group UK Ltd.
UKHW050239220624
444555UK00005BA/451